Exceeding Expectations

EXCEEDING EXPECTATIONS

Reflections on Leadership

General Bill Looney

USAF (Ret.)

◯

Enso Books

...because ideas matter

United States of America

Requests for permissions should be sent to Enso Books, Shakespeare Station, P.O. Box 230603, Montgomery, Alabama, 36123 or by e-mail to *permissions@ensobooks.com*.

Enso Books offers discounts on its titles when ordered in bulk for training, educational or fund-raising purposes. For more information, please contact the publisher directly by e-mail at *sales@ensobooks.com* or visit *www.ensobooks.com*.

Company names and slogans mentioned herein are the trademarks or registered trademarks of their respective owners. Credits appear in the ***Acknowledgements***.

While the publisher and the author have used their best efforts in preparing this book, they make no representations or warranties with respect to the accuracy or completeness of the contents of this book and specifically disclaim any implied warranties of merchantability or fitness for a particular purpose. No warranty may be created or extended by sales representatives or written sales materials.

Author photograph by Joel Martinez. Cover designed by Deanne Driver. All images reprinted with permission.

Cataloguing-in-Publication Data

Looney, William R., III, 1949-
Exceeding expectations: reflections on leadership / 1st ed.
174 p., 21 cm.
IBSN: 978-0-9820185-1-4 (paperback)
1. Leadership   I. Title: Exceeding expectations.   II. Title

HD57.7.F444 2009   LCCN: 2009925001
658.4'092-dc22

Printed in the United States of America

Dedication

This book is dedicated to leaders who create organizations to *exceed expectations!*

In Gratitude

To my wife, Marilyn, and children, Erika and Meredith, whose love, support, and sacrifices have let me "live my dream."

TABLE OF CONTENTS

—◦◊◦—

Introduction

Other than religion, sex, and politics, leadership may be the most discussed subject in the world. The reason is very simple – without effective leadership, very little happens; with effective leadership, anything can happen. Whether you are leading military forces into battle, directing a business, coaching an athletic team, or leading a nation; effective, motivating, and inspiring leadership is the key to success.

In today's world, organizations seek out people who can lead and motivate their workforce to *exceed expectations*. These leaders will be the superstars of this generation. They will not only inspire and motivate us to meet goals, but they will also go far beyond surpassing the expectations of senior leadership. The individual who can lead in this manner will be highly sought after and rewarded. By applying the lessons of this book, I hope to show you the tools used by this exciting group of emerging leaders of leaders.

Looking back upon my career culminating as a four-star general, I realize I learned almost everything I needed to know about leadership at the squadron level. Much like that book about learning everything we needed to know about life in kindergarten, I believe the same thing is true about a person's first real leadership opportunity. Why? Because in your first real leadership experience, you are often closer to both your boss and your followers than you will ever be in future leadership roles. Follow-on opportunities will typically move you further up the leadership chain and farther away from the people who "make it happen." In your first leadership role, you will likely see and experience how your leadership style is perceived by others. Are you comfortable in your role? Do you relate well to your people? Do they respect you? Do you create an environment of trust and confidence? Does your organization not only get the job done, but also exceed expectations?

I dedicated my entire life to leading others and experienced the art of leadership at every organizational level. In the pages that follow, I hope to share with you some of the lessons I observed. It is important to note that these are observations, not absolute principles. Nevertheless, I believe the lessons here have great potential to serve as a guide to success.

In my personal experience, I have found that discussing leadership approaches is interesting but not enduring. Discussions about leadership are soon forgotten, but stories about people aren't. We may not remember a lecture or a book, but we often remember stories we heard. And that's what this book is – a compilation of real stories about real people in real situations. Some are funny, others are sad, but they are all real. These are not hypothetical scenarios but actual leadership situations with real world results. Hopefully, you will find a few instructive, if not inspiring.

No matter how much you might talk about leadership or how many approaches you may study, you will eventually have to embrace a style of leadership which best suits your strengths. It is critical for you to feel comfortable in your style or else your followers may perceive your leadership abilities as shallow or superficial. My best advice is to be yourself and discover what you believe to be most important to become the type of leader you envision for yourself. Hopefully, the stories I recount here might help you reflect as you continue on your own leadership journey. It goes without saying, what worked for me may not suit your style, and that's okay. After all, a leadership style reflects a person's beliefs and comfort level.

Leadership is leadership regardless of your position in an organization. No matter whether you are a unit commander, shift superintendent, division chief or a team captain, your first task should always be to build an organizational culture that will motivate and inspire others to exceed expectations. Your goal should never be to meet them. Many leaders can meet expectations, but what I have continually seen from my perspective as a career officer and general is that the best and most successful leaders always exceed them.

Highly effective leaders who exceed expectations do so through follower performance, unit performance, and personal performance. All three elements must work in harmony if *exceeding expectations* is to be the *norm* rather than the exception. Leadership is the key to all three areas. Followers need to be inspired and motivated to reach a higher level instead of settling for a "good enough" mentality. This is where the leader's personal commitment demonstrated by his or her actions influences follower performance. Whether it be through the manner in which you engage your followers, a humble yet forthright approach, or the empathy you feel when you exhibit the ability "to walk in their shoes," followers must first feel a leader's commitment before they make a commitment of their own. Without commitment, exceeding expectations is very difficult, if not impossible.

Organizations require standards, decisiveness, and clarity of purpose to thrive and excel. Without an organizational environment where all members feel free from discrimination, harassment, intimidation, or favoritism, it is impossible for the followers to reach their full performance potential. The leader is the key. Leaders create organizational environments with their vision, and enforcement of standards that allows the workforce to excel. Along with standards and their enforcement is the need for timely and well-reasoned decisions. Without quality decision making, organizations essentially stall out. Followers are ready to follow, and they are eagerly looking to you as the leader to make decisions. They'll do the work, but they'll need you as the leader to make good decisions and point them to success.

Finally, the personal performance of the leader creates the final element propelling followers and organizations to exceed expectations. Leaders must reach deep inside themselves to do "the right thing." Such actions as leading from the front, maintaining the highest levels of integrity regardless of consequences, or taking risks on your followers' behalf are all actions that inspire and motivate. In most cases, this type of leader behavior usually exceeds the expectations followers have for their leader. In the following pages, I hope to share with you some of my observations, thoughts and reflections that will allow you to create an organizational environment where exceeding expectations is the norm, not the exception!

A Leadership Perspective

As I begin this discussion on leadership, I believe it is paramount to first address the leader's perspective. By that, I'm referring to how a leader views himself or herself in relation to those they lead. Such self-awareness is crucial because this view will color or influence every facet of the leader.

Unfortunately, the environment we grow up in doesn't always create the right perspective. Every organization we belong to from Boy Scouts, athletic

teams, clubs or college sororities always has an organization chart. Invariably the chart looks like a pyramid with all the appropriate positions listed.

At the bottom of the chart is the majority of the membership, and as you move up the pyramid there are fewer positions until you arrive at the top where only one position resides – the leader.

The chart is a helpful depiction of the organizational structure, but it also has a tendency to promote a subliminal message to all who see it. The perceived message is the person on top is the most important person in the organization. Some viewers infer the "other people" in the org chart are there for only one reason – to make the leader successful so that the organization will be successful. When you add the perks and special privileges accorded to the leader's position, it's easy to see how this position could be viewed as the most crucial to success. Unfortunately, many cues silently scream out that the organization is all about the leader. Nothing could be further from the truth.

Sadly, I came to learn that leaders who lack a certain level of self-awareness are at risk of adopting this perspective once they arrive at the top. After all, the organizational chart clearly shows their position over everyone else. Therefore, when these individuals achieve a leadership position, it is no wonder they take on an air of entitlement, and a perspective that "this is all about me!" My experience has shown me that this is exactly the wrong perspective to embrace. It is usually a recipe for disaster or, at the very least, poor performance from the organization.

The leader should embrace a perspective that turns the organizational pyramid upside down with the sub-

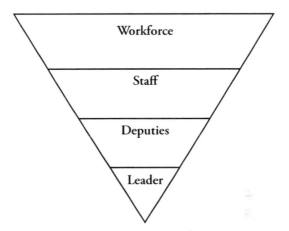

ordinates on top and the leader on the bottom. What this perspective says loud and clear is that it is "all about the people, not just the leader!" Although the leader is a key component with significant authority and responsibility, it takes everyone to accomplish an organization's mission. The leader may have the vision and set the course, but it takes everyone to turn a vision into a reality. With this perspective, a leader learns to appreciate how his primary role is enabling other people because their performance determines success or failure. When a leader embraces this perspective, he or she is more concerned with the welfare of the workforce, both from a personal and professional aspect, than their own status as a leader. No longer is the leader concerned with perks, fanfare, and special attention, but more about worker welfare.

Their leadership perspective is quickly noted by the workforce. The leader who believes "it is all about me" and expects special treatment will quickly lose the commitment of the followers. This lack of workforce commitment will likely result in a "meeting the standard" approach to performance. The leader who puts workers first will quickly develop a bond with them that will create an environment where exceeding expectations is the norm, not the exception.

In the following chapters, I share my experiences as I strived to create an environment that was about the workers and not me as the leader. These efforts consistently resulted in performance that exceeded expectations – and not in just one organization, but in every organization I had an opportunity to lead. Although *exceeding expectations* is always a challenging goal, it is achievable with the correct leadership perspective. The leader needs to not only appreciate but embrace the concept that "it's all about *them, not me!*" Some leaders recognize this quickly and pile up success after success, while others struggle and fail to realize their leader-centered approach is not connecting with those that depend upon them. After forty years of being up close and personal with leadership, I guarantee you that this perspective succeeds every time.

Humility, Humility, Humility

Humility is an attribute which typically isn't among the top traits people suggest when defining the qualities necessary for successful leadership. However, my experience has taught me how essential humility is in keeping leaders grounded and aware of their own human frailties. Humility allows leaders to remain connected with their followers on a level that allows frank and candid interchange. When leaders begin to believe they are somehow above their followers, they end up as haughty, aloof, out of touch and ineffective.

In the military, probably more so than in other organizations, it is very easy to fall prey to the pomp and circumstance associated with command. With requirements for people to rise when the commander enters the room to the unique flags, uniforms, and music associated with a command, it is easy to understand how this could all go to a leader's head. Unfortunately, it is one of the biggest mistakes any leader makes, and it usually spells disaster for both the leader and the organization. Leaders who fall victim to this self-adulation usually find it hard to accept advice, consult with others when making decisions, ask for inputs, and, most importantly, admit personal mistakes and accept responsibility, These characteristics are all crucial for a leader to earn the respect, trust and confidence from their followers.

A Drive Home

One of my most vivid experiences that helped remind me not to take myself too seriously occurred during my tour at Langley as the 1st Fighter Wing commander. At the end of the workday, I left the office to pick up my personal car from the base service station after having some work completed. I asked my executive officer to drive with me over to the garage and drop me off. We drove my Air Force staff car that was painted a distinctive blue with a white top. This is done so the airmen can easily tell when the wing commander is passing by and render proper courtesies – usually a salute.

As we drove over to the garage, a number of individuals stopped to salute, wave, smile, or otherwise acknowledge my presence and position. A few passing motorists even waved or honked a greeting. These nice gestures on their part let me know they had noticed me. This is the kind of behavior that Air Force tradition and protocol prescribe when a commander drives by in the official staff car.

Upon arriving at the garage, I paid my bill and began to drive my personal car home. My exec took the staff car back to the office. The drive home was entirely different from the drive to the garage. Even though I was in a sharp red convertible, not one individual noticed me. Not one salute, not one wave, not even a slight nod. As a matter of fact, I think a young airman yelled at me when he thought I cut him off at an intersection. How quickly things change…

My initial reaction was one of amusement, but the more I thought about it, the more I realized there was a great lesson here for all that aspired to leadership. The lesson was quite simple: always take your position seriously and expect the proper courtesies, but never take *yourself* too seriously. When I drove to the garage in my staff car, I was the 1st Fighter Wing commander, and the troops paid the respect the *position* deserved. However, when I jumped into my red convertible for the drive home, all anyone saw was just another person heading home after a long day. There was no requirement to salute or acknowledge my presence; after all, I really was not in any official role as the commander on the drive home in my personal car. I was the commander on the way to the garage, and I was just Bill Looney on the way home.

A humble leader realizes that all the ruffle and flourishes, salutes, special offices and staffs are there as a reflection of the importance of the office, *not* the individual holding the office at that time. With that realization it becomes easy to determine what actions are proper for one's role as the leader, and what one should rightfully expect as just another human being on this Earth.

Unfortunately, I have seen quite a few commanders who believed all the pomp and circumstance was entirely appropriate because they saw themselves as a special, unique person deserving of such regard. They came to expect such treatment no matter their position, and made life miserable for those who had to work with them. These leaders assumed they were all-knowing, always right, and chosen in some special way above all others. Some even went so far as to assume an imperial air, and hold court like a king or monarch. Such individuals did not inspire or motivate their followers to achieve at high levels and exceed expectations. On the contrary, the minimum often became good enough.

Such a leader will receive very little counsel when making decisions when his manner conveys there is no need for such input. Most importantly, such a leader will also usually have a difficult time admitting a mistake or accepting less than perfect performance. During the same tour at Langley, I discovered how much the airmen appreciate humility in their leadership.

The Base Theater

The Air Force had experienced several unprofessional incidents within our medical corps – doctors having affairs with patients and nurses, officers dating enlisted members, and on and on. The Surgeon General decided one of his remedies to this mess was to stand down the entire medical corps and have a day of briefings and discussions on professional conduct. The medical group commander asked if I would start the discussions off with a short introduction about the importance of professionalism. I agreed and was more than happy to participate because as the wing commander, I had a vested interest in the medical group's morale and performance.

The briefing was held in the base theater, and as I entered, the airmen were customarily called to attention. I asked them to take their seats and then began my remarks. A few minutes into my talk, I noticed an individual about halfway up the rows of seats appeared to be reading a paper or magazine. Although this lack of respect and common courtesy bothered me, I usually ignored it in situations where I was speaking to a large group. I realized if I reprimanded the individual in front of the group I would probably lose my audience. Some would wonder what the individual was doing, others would consider it poor form to correct someone in public, and many would just tune me out. In the end, I would have lost their attention and the whole purpose for making the remarks would have been wasted.

However, this time I could not stop myself. This was the third briefing I had given in the previous two days, and I had already put up with a few people sleeping. Even though I had gotten my message across to the majority of my audience, it still grated on me. I stopped in mid-sentence, pointed to the individual, told him to put his paper down, and pay attention to what I was saying in a loud and correcting tone. The result was exactly as I predicted. The entire room sat up, became extremely quiet, and tuned me out. I realized this was the case, and shortly thereafter concluded my remarks and, of course, received no questions.

Everyone appeared eager for me to leave and their commander was visibly upset over the individual's actions. The room came to attention, and as I departed, you could have heard a pin drop. I was unhappy with myself for succumbing to my frustration and regretted my action, even though many would say it was justified. As I entered the lobby to exit the theater, a senior medical officer approached me and identified himself as the culprit.

Before I had a chance to make a comment, he went on to explain his actions. First, he showed me the paper he was supposedly reading – it turned out to be a loose-leaf notebook. Then he showed me an area in the notebook where he had taken notes on my briefing. His explanation was that he had heard I was a great speaker, and wanted to take notes to share with his airmen that were unable to attend the session.

I was already feeling badly about my outburst, and now I felt absolutely horrible. He graciously accepted my profuse apologies, and went back into the auditorium. I left the theater, and got into my staff car, but I could not turn the key and start the engine. I just kept going over in my mind how I had publicly humiliated an innocent individual and how horrible I felt about my behavior.

I took the key out of ignition, got out of the car, and went back into the theater. This time no one was expecting me, so the airmen were not called to attention. As I made my way down the aisle, individuals noticing me began to stand and it became like a wave at a football stadium. I'm sure everyone in the audience was bracing themselves for an encore to my early admonishment. As I reached the stage, the medical group commander also had a shocked and concerned look on his face since he didn't know why I had returned.

I immediately asked everyone to take their seats, and then I stated to the audience that a few minutes earlier I had publicly reprimanded an individual in their unit. Since that time, I had come to find out that my reprimand was not justified. Additionally, I realized that since I had made this reprimand in front of his peers and subordinates, I had caused this individual needless embarrassment and humiliation. Therefore, it was only fair that I should publicly apologize to this individual in front of the same audience. After stating my sincere apology, I departed the stage.

As I began to walk up the aisle, the troops began to stand, and then they began to clap, and then whistle, and cheer. I'll have to admit I never expected such a response nor will I ever forget the chill up and down my spine and the tearing in my eyes. I had made a serious error, I had admitted it, and the airmen had accepted my apology. All was forgiven.

From that day forth, neither my family members nor I could go in the hospital without being greeted by so many well wishers. The service we received was absolutely fantastic. Granted, wing commanders always get great service, but this was a little more special and reflected a true feeling of warmth and affection. To this day, I occasionally run into some individuals who were there that day and they remind me how much my apology impressed them.

What impressed the airmen was that their leader – a senior commander – made a mistake and was willing to publicly admit it and make it right. Some that say commanders can never admit to mistakes – to do so erodes confidence in their leadership. I vehemently disagree. To err is human, and leaders are human. Leaders make mistakes. When they attempt to cover them up, or act as though no one noticed, they only fool themselves. They also lose the respect of their followers, and in some extreme cases gain their contempt.

Although a leader cannot survive by consistently making bad decisions and using poor judgment, all leaders make mistakes. The difference is between those who accept responsibility and make amends, and the others who feel any admission is a sign of weakness.

As a follower, give me the leader who recognizes his own mistakes, because that leader will be receptive to advice and understand when others make mistakes. Such an approach will go a long way to building trust, confidence, and teamwork.

Whether you lead in the military or the private sector, you are subject to the worst disease a leader can get – arrogance. Once you begin to feel you are personally deserving of all the special treatment and attention, you are headed for trouble. You will find when you assume a position of leadership, even in a small organization, everyone smiles at you. Everyone values your opinion. Your jokes are funnier. You look great in everything you wear. Special attention only increases the higher you go in the leadership chain.

This is human nature. First, it is natural that workers want to please their boss since their future and fortune usually is determined by that person. Second, when confronted with all the special attention, it is also understandable how a leader begins to believe he or she is somehow better than everyone else. There is very little a leader can do about the first, but a lot the leader can do about the second. Just remember, "*it's the position, not me*," and you'll do just fine.

When it comes to expectations, humility is not one most followers expect their leaders to have. This isn't to say followers expect their leader to be arrogant, withdrawn, and untouchable. However, it is probably fair to say that most followers do not expect their leader to be a "regular" guy – and by regular I do not mean that the leader is their "buddy," but rather someone who is approachable, positive, appreciative, and most of all aware of his or her own imperfections and willing to acknowledge, apologize, and correct his failings.

This requirement is sometimes a tall order for a leader, especially one who is taken with his position and own self importance. This type of leader sometimes meets followers' expectations, but will never exceed them. On the other hand, the leader who regards a sense of humility as a cornerstone of his leadership philosophy will almost certainly exceed expectations – and is well on the way to creating a culture poised for success.

LEAD FROM THE FRONT

You would be amazed at how many individuals, when given the opportunity to lead an organization, fail to lead. I'm not sure whether it's because they are unsure of their capabilities, their role, or are just unwilling to assume the responsibilities required of a leader.

I have found when leaders fail to lead, the organization essentially comes to a standstill. The unit makes absolutely no progress. After all, the main reason an individual is selected to be the leader is to lead the organization to even higher levels of achievement and productivity.

Rescuing the Boat People

When I was a newly promoted lieutenant colonel, I became the operations officer (second in command) of a fighter squadron at Bitburg Air Base, Germany. Unfortunately, the squadron I was assigned to was the worst of three fighter squadrons in our wing. Morale was low, and performance was even worse. At the Officers' Club on Friday night, one usually heard the young lieutenants and captains complaining about the absolute lack of leadership demonstrated by their commander, and the resulting poor reputation the squadron held within the wing. The young officers had even named themselves the "Boat People" – a reference to the refugees who had fled Vietnam and floated aimlessly in the South China Sea awaiting rescue. From their perspective, they were just like the boat people: adrift, without a direction or purpose, waiting for someone to rescue them.

I reported to the squadron on a late Friday afternoon, and had a chance to talk with a few of the young officers. I had met them earlier during my time at Bitburg, but had not come to know them very well. There was an excitement in the squadron because they were preparing to deploy to Zaragoza Air Base in Spain for some combat training against F-16s. Deploying to another location for training is a common occurrence for a fighter squadron. It is usually done to allow units to fly where the weather is better and get them away from the everyday demands at home base so they can focus on combat flying training. It was natural for these young officers to be excited about going to Spain to fly against F-16s and enjoy good times together. Additionally, it also gave them an opportunity to check out their new operations officer – *me*.

We took ten aircraft and fifteen pilots. The commander stayed behind at home base and allowed me to take the deployment so I could get to know the pilots. The flight down to "Zaz," as we commonly referred to Zaragoza, was uneventful. Shortly after we landed we began a series of briefings on the local area and safety considerations. At the conclusion of the briefings, the pilots gathered together to discuss the next day's activities and plans for the deployment. In the meantime, the scheduler began to post the flying schedule for the next day. The first mission of the day would be a "4v4" against F-16s. A "4v4" (four versus four) involves eight aircraft divided into two groups of four that fly mock combat against each other. In this case, we would fly our four F-15s against four F-16s.

Until this point, the squadron commander had opted not to lead any 4v4 missions for two reasons. He did not possess the flying skills or proficiency required to lead such a demanding mission. Even worse, he wasn't willing to put in the effort required to plan, brief, lead, and debrief this type of mission. This was a sore point with all the lieutenants and captains, and led to their complete lack of respect for him as a commander.

As the scheduler started to put names against the missions, he asked me who would lead the next morning's 4v4. Almost on cue, the entire room grew quiet as each pilot listened for my response. I stated in a fairly straightforward manner that I would be "Number One" for the next day's mission. The room remained silent for a few moments more. A few of the pilots exchanged glances, and then went back to their discussions. I assumed what each individual was thinking – while they expected me to step forward and take the lead, they also wondered whether or not I could deliver. I have to admit that I was also a little anxious. I wasn't worried about whether or not I could deliver – after all, I had been flying the F-15 almost six years and had accumulated over 1,000 hours in the aircraft. I had been an instructor pilot in previous units and had led numerous 4v4 missions. I was worried about earning the respect of this particular group of pilots.

The flying business is a demanding and complex environment where many factors that you have absolutely no control over can sometimes influence your performance. A faulty radar, difficult weather conditions, or airplane problems can turn a routine mission into an absolute nightmare. I spent most of the night tossing and turning thinking of the myriad of situations which could ruin the mission. I also realized that this was my first opportunity to lead these young officers and everything was on the line. Once you lose their respect, it takes forever to regain it – if you are ever able to do so.

I was up bright and early to check the status of the weather. The sun was shining and there was not a cloud in the sky. My spirits immediately soared, and I hoped this was a good omen of things to come. I arrived at the squadron a good two hours before the briefing to review and prepare. I had already put together my briefing the afternoon prior. It took hours to put together a professional brief that covered the blackboard with the mission objectives, rules of engagement, mission roles, and other information critical to the flight briefing. Pilots tended to judge each other by the effort they put into their briefs. Thus, almost all flight leaders put their briefs up the day prior if they had an early morning flight.

I had observed that working hard on a brief and doing it well tended to set the tone for the entire mission. If you had your act together the flight tended to go well. On the other hand, it usually followed that a poor brief resulted in a below average flight. When a senior officer, especially a commander, began to believe that their seniority and position no longer required the same effort to prepare a brief, they quickly lost respect in the eyes of the young pilots. It was clear to me that an effective leader could never let this happen.

Thanks to my prior preparation, the brief went well. I could tell the pilots appreciated the effort I had put into the brief, and were comfortable with my ability to brief what appeared to be a reasonable plan. Now it was time to suit up and go to our aircraft. This part of the mission I had absolutely no control over. I had to count on my maintenance airmen to provide us with four fully mission capable jets – and that they did. Believe me, I have been a part of many a mission that went south just because one of the four aircraft had a bad radar. So far, so good.

Start, taxi, and take off went smoothly. We climbed up into the early morning sunrise ready to tackle four F-16s. For this mission, the F-16s were to play the role of the MiGs, or "Red Force" while the F-15s were the good guys, or "Blue Force." The F-15 versus F-16 rivalry was intense but good-natured, between the two communities. However, the last thing you would ever want to do is lose an aircraft playing the role of a MiG.

In order to train realistically, the Blue Force would require the Red Force to replicate the capabilities of the real-world Soviet threat. Although the Soviets possessed capable aircraft, their aircraft in no way compared to an F-15 or an F-16. Therefore, the advantage was always on the Blue side before the fight began. However, if the Blue team made a critical mistake, the Red team could make them pay dearly.

Although I had been anxious about my performance during this particular flight from the minute it went on the scheduling board, the instant I commanded "*fight's on*" over the radio, I no longer had time to worry. The two four-ships were initially separated by about sixty nautical miles, but when you're both flying at speeds between 600 to 700 nautical miles per hour, the distance closes pretty quickly.

The Soviets respected the capability of the F-15 radar to determine the number of aircraft in a formation, and realized to defeat it, a flight of MiGs needed to stay close together until they arrived between 10-15 miles from a flight of F-15s. At that point, the MiGs would wildly split away from one another in all different directions. This tactic's purpose was to get one or two MiGs into the fight untargeted.

It takes great discipline and proficiency by each pilot of an F-15 four ship to ensure that all the MiGs are targeted. The closer you get, the higher the tension builds, and unless each member of the flight follows his or her assigned task, a MiG usually gets in untargeted. We expected the F-16s to replicate this tactic, and were determined to target all four.

As we ran in on this particular setup, we had accounted for three of the four F-16s at fifteen miles out, but were still missing one. The closer we got, the more anxious I became knowing that situations such as this could spell disaster for the Blue Force. Suddenly, my wingman confirmed over the radio he had found and targeted the fourth MiG. With all four MiGs targeted we quickly killed them, and returned back to our side of the flying area.

We had enough gas for one more setup, and it went as smoothly as the first. I was ecstatic and relieved that the mission had gone so well. I knew that some luck was involved in our success. We had great weather, great airplanes, and full up radars on our side – not an everyday occurrence. Yet, I also realized we had a good plan going in and we had followed it. The results were precisely what we had set out to do – a clean sweep of the F-16s.

After we landed and returned to the squadron, we began the debrief. This is yet another area the commander and some other senior pilots let slide in the past. The former commander had never debriefed because he never led, and while some of the senior pilots did lead, they tended to slight the debrief. Like the initial brief, a good debrief takes a considerable amount of effort if you desire a professional and beneficial outcome.

An in-depth, worthwhile debrief after a 4v4 mission usually takes two to three hours depending on the complexity of the mission. Of all the facets of the training mission – the briefing, the flight, and the debrief – the debrief is the most important. Here, you are able to determine what went right, and what went wrong, and why. This is where the real learning takes place, and the young pilots looked forward to these debriefs to identify their shortcomings and gain an insight into performance improvement.

Those in leadership roles who make the debrief an objective, candid assessment that highlights positives and negatives along with ways to improve gain tremendous respect from those they lead. Pilots who never debriefed or led a poorly organized, unprofessional debriefs are almost never respected within a squadron.

By the end of the debrief, it seemed pretty clear that I had established my credibility and leadership role within the squadron. In my mind, it began with my willingness to lead. Although, it did cause some anxious moments for me, the respect and credibility I gained by being the leader far outweighed the risk I took as they saw it. I had set out to exceed everyone's expectations and had been successful.

Squadrons are typically created equally in terms of numbers of superstars, above average performers, average performers, and every now and then, a slacker. The difference between a *good* and a *great* squadron always boils down to the leader. Leaders that were respected and led from the front inspired and motivated their people to new heights of achievement. When I arrived at Bitburg, the 22nd Fighter Squadron not only was considered to be the worst squadron in the wing, but quite possibly the worst in the Air Force. Two years later, that squadron had been recognized twice as the best fighter squadron in Europe, and had also been selected as the best air-to-air squadron in the Air Force. Certainly, I was not uniquely responsible for the squadron's success. On the contrary, the squadron's men, women, and their families, working as a team, made all that happen. However, like any organization, the squadron required a leader to point it in the direction of success and achievement.

The lesson from this experience applies across all leadership positions: when placed in charge, lead from the front, not the rear. Your subordinates will always look for you to show them the way, and to prove you are qualified to be their leader. Even though "leading from the front" continues to be a basic tenet of leadership, it still amazes me how many leaders fail to grasp it.

Yet, what is even more amazing is how many followers do not expect their leaders to take the point. *Why?* Quite simply because followers understand there is an inherent risk of failure when you lead from the front. Many followers assume their leaders are adverse to any risk that would put their future success in jeopardy. This is a sad but often true statement. I have seen it play out over and over again in my experience. For the leader who is willing to accept the risk and step to the front, the opportunity to exceed your followers' expectations is waiting to be seized. Regardless of the outcome, the simple fact you stepped forward will always be appreciated by your followers.

It is also important to recognize that you don't have to *always* lead from the front in every situation. Leaders also have a responsibility to give their subordinates opportunities to grow and enhance their leadership skills by taking the lead. What is important is that your followers know you can lead from the front because you have successfully demonstrated it over and over again. If you have done so, you have most likely exceeded their expectations and created in them the desire to raise the bar even higher.

Risk And Return

For those who have studied the art of leadership, setting the example is an approach which is readily understood and appreciated. While this is true, there are many leaders who believe setting an example is rather easy. My experience has taught me otherwise. In order to set a proper example, the leader has to be willing to take on the same challenges and accept the same risk as his or her followers.

Too often, some leaders are willing to merely do the superficial, and settle for "good enough" when it comes to setting an example. There are those in the military who think having a haircut within limits, a clean and pressed uniform and shiny shoes are the main ingredients for setting the proper leadership example. I'm the first to agree a sharp and crisp outward appearance sets the right tone for a leader. However, it's not enough. Appearance is superficial. Subordinates look for something more substantial than outward appearance when it comes to an example. Subordinates want to know that the boss is willing to do the same task he asks them to perform and take the same risks when he issues an order.

For a leader to set the proper example, he or she must be willing to inconvenience themselves and accept risk. When I became the commander of the Air Force's training command as a four-star general,

I became one of a select few. With all the attention and extra "help" I received, it would have been easy to think of myself as "special" and excuse myself from doing what I required of others. After all, everyone knew I could do it if I wanted to, and not everything that applied to my followers should necessarily apply to me. *Wrong! Wrong! Wrong!* This approach, which I have observed in more than one senior leader, will undoubtedly destroy a leader's credibility.

Buckle Up: It's Not What You Think

During my time in the training command, I drove myself to work since I lived close to the headquarters. More than once, I found myself in a hurry to get to the office, and as I would start to roll forward in my car I would realize I had not buckled my seat belt. My first thought was "What does it matter? It's only a five minute drive." Additionally, I doubted anyone would report me for not buckling up. After all, I was a four-star general. But then I would remind myself,

> *What are you thinking, Bill? You are the commander. If someone sees you they will not know whether you've been driving for five minutes or five hours. All they will know is that you are the commander and you are not wearing your seat belt. Then they'll wonder how many other things you don't do but require of others.*

With that admonition, I would buckle my seat belt and drive on.

This story illustrates how you must demand as much of yourself as a leader as you will demand of your followers – no matter how inconsequential the action may seem. It doesn't matter whether you agree with the rule, it is the rule, and you are expected to set the example by following it. Leaders who place themselves above rules and policies set themselves up for failure and loss of credibility. Personal commitment to safe actions can save lives. You can preach aircraft safety all day, but if you start taking shortcuts on the little things like buckling up, you're probably not *committed* to safety. Thus, can you really expect it of anyone else from a pilot to a school-age child crossing the street? It's not so much about the buckle as it is about holding yourself to your own expectations. You must walk the talk, even if no one is looking. Little things matter.

Setting the example not only requires leaders to follow the rules but also requires them to accept risk when it is not necessarily required of them to do so. By accepting the risk and putting yourself in the same situation as your followers, your actions will generate tremendous respect for and commitment to you.

The Test of the Test

As a squadron commander, I can still vividly remember my first major inspection. At that time, every inspection included a written test administered to the squadron pilots. The inspection team realized it was difficult to schedule each and every pilot to take the test at the same time, so they only required a squadron to produce sixty percent of their pilots for the test. This requirement has since changed and most Air Force commands require all pilots to test.

In all the inspections I had seen in past assignments, I noticed this percentage was typically made up of lieutenants and captains. You seldom saw a major in the group, much less a lieutenant colonel – and certainly never a squadron commander or operations officer. Senior officers presumably had much more important things to do than take a test with young pilots.

In reality, these individuals were reluctant to take the test. From their perspective, there was absolutely nothing to gain by passing the test with a high score, but there was a lot to lose if you failed. There was even one squadron back in the States, where both the commander and operations officer went on leave during the inspection so they would not have to take the test and be subjected to the risk of failure. You can imagine how well that went over with the younger officers they left behind to carry the load.

This practice had always irritated me and flew in the face of setting the proper leadership example. I made a vow to myself years earlier that if I ever became a squadron commander, I would make sure that I not only tested, but so would every senior leader in my squadron, along with all my pilots. One month prior to the inspection, I brought all the squadron pilots together and told them that not only I, but every pilot would take the test, and I would match my score against their score for beers.

On the surface, this could sound like a very difficult challenge for a squadron commander to take on. After all, the commander is typically much busier than most of the people who work for him. And as I mentioned earlier, there was supposedly nothing to be gained by testing, only hell to pay if you busted and lowered the overall squadron average. However, I believed there was a lot to be gained by a commander who was willing to take the risk.

As it turned out, the risk was minimal. The test was taken from a bank of 500 questions, and all one had to do was dedicate the time to memorize the questions and answers. This only took about an hour or two of concentrated effort with a little follow-up review in the time leading up to the test. I believe the real issue with commanders who had not tested before was that they were just too lazy – too lazy to dedicate those few hours to prepare for a simple, straight-forward, test.

The test was held in the wing auditorium with all three squadrons participating. Each squadron sat together as a group in a particular section of the room. As the room began to fill prior to the start time, it became very apparent that our squadron not only had the largest number of pilots testing, but that number also included the squadron commander and operations officer.

As the test began, you could sense the pride within our squadron as our pilots looked at the other units and realized that those squadrons could barely make their sixty percent requirement and their squadron leadership was nowhere in sight. At the same time, you could feel the disappointment in the other squadrons' pilots as they reflected on their poor showing, and more importantly, the lack of involvement by their leadership. Both of these feelings, one of pride by our pilots, and the other, disappointment and envy the other squadrons' pilots had for our squadron, certainly fired up our people and impressed the inspectors. Preparing for the test really wasn't that big of a challenge. In fact, I only missed two on the test and had one of the low scores. The majority of everyone else scored 100 percent and I had to pay up.

What emerged from this experience was the fact that when followers realized their leader was going to take the test with them, accept the same risk of a possible low score and the embarrassment which could follow, there was no way they were going to get a low score and let either him or their peers down. This quest for testing excellence helped our squadron build a commitment to putting forth our best effort not only on that test, but also in every other facet of that inspection. As you might imagine, not only did we have the highest participation in the wing, but we also achieved the highest scores.

In addition to the test, each squadron was also given a flying evaluation which was far more difficult. There is a lot more to a flying evaluation than just sitting down and providing answers to questions in an air conditioned, no-stress environment. If you were a flight lead, which most commanders were, then you were evaluated on your ability to plan a mission, brief the mission, lead the flight, and debrief the results. There were a lot of opportunities to make mistakes. I witnessed the same pattern as I had observed in the testing area. Commanders tended to shy away from ever taking a flight evaluation during an inspection. In their minds this was just an opportunity to fail, and should be avoided at all costs.

The system itself made it easy for commanders to avoid receiving a flight check. All the flight evaluators were young majors and captains who had previously served in F-15 units. Although they had absolutely no reluctance in failing a peer whose performance was substandard, they were very reluctant to do the same to a senior officer or commander. This was understandable. After all, these young officers hoped to come back to operational units and have a chance to compete for a leadership position. It certainly would not improve their chances if they were to fail one of the sitting commanders during an inspection. Over the course of fifteen years, I had never seen a commander selected for a flight check unless he requested one. I felt compelled to change the leadership approach now that I was in a position to do so.

The inspection began on Monday morning with a briefing to the inspection team in our squadron conference room. After the briefing, I asked the flight evaluators to accompany me to the scheduling office. Once there, I took them over to the scheduling board that laid out all of the week's flight activities for the squadron. Each mission was clearly displayed for each day of the week. I told the evaluators they were free to choose any mission and pilot they would like to fly with except in one case. Before the evaluators could fly with any of my pilots, they would have to fly with me. I was scheduled to lead a mission the next morning.

As soon as a word spread that the boss was going to fly the first check, you could sense a feeling of pride and confidence surge through the squadron. It had nothing to do with my aviation skills, but rather the fact I was willing to put myself at risk just like the rest of the pilots selected to take a check. Plus, I had also let the evaluators pick with whom they wanted to fly instead of scheduling them with our best pilots. This also sent a clear message that I trusted each and every one of them to fly a great check ride if called upon.

I appreciated the risk I was taking, but I also realized that my chance of failure was far less than my chance of success. After all, I had years of experience in the air-to-air fighter business and knew I possessed the proficiency to pass the check. Of course, there still was no doubt in my mind if I did something really dumb or made a gross safety violation, the inspector would fail me.

The next day, I showed up early to prepare for the flight. The briefing, the flight, and the debrief went very well, and I passed the check with a strong performance. I knew it didn't have to be the best check ride the inspector had ever evaluated, but I strived to do my very best. I did not want to put him in a position where he felt pressured to pass me if my performance did not warrant a passing grade. The only sure way to make this happen was to exceed the expectations I had set for myself.

After my flight, ten other pilots of the squadron took their checks. I had gone first not because I was under any illusion that I was the best pilot in the squadron, but simply believed I had to set the proper example by putting myself at risk first. Again, we all received high passing grades – and the highest check ride scores in the wing.

Without the willingness to take risk, a person becomes little more than a machine; only making decisions when it is so obvious a child could pick the right course of action. I have found that the risks I took as a leader usually fell into two categories – risks

I took relying on my personal performance, and risks I took relying on my people.

It is easier to take risks when the only variable involved is your personal performance than it is when you are relying on your people to perform as advertised. However, for a leader, the payoff for taking risks involving your people is much greater than any successful personal performance. Additionally, individuals not willing to put their personal performance at risk are usually very reluctant to ever entrust their personal fate to their people.

Taking risks with your people is an entirely different proposition. First, you will have very little control over the outcome – your people will. Second, what influence you bring to bear on their performance will be based on their respect for you and your position. Finally, whatever is achieved will be a shared victory vice an individual one for the leader. I've had many experiences taking risks by trusting my people to do the right thing, but two experiences especially illustrate this point.

General Order #1

During my command of the 33rd Fighter Wing at Eglin AFB in Florida, our country decided to invade Haiti in an operation called Uphold Democracy. Our wing was to act as the lead organization for about 60 aircraft and 1,000 personnel which would participate in the invasion. The plan was to deploy to Roosevelt Roads Naval Air Station in Puerto Rico and then fly missions in support of the Haiti invasion.

There were many who wondered why the U.S. deployed so many aircraft to support an invasion against a small, Third World country which hardly had an air force, much less presented a threat to our forces. In reality, our concern was not with Haiti, but a possible intervention by Cuba and their air force. Losing a transport, loaded with Army paratroopers, to a Cuban MiG would have been a political disaster for the administration, and would have reflected very poorly on our military.

I was very fortunate to have had this command opportunity and looked forward to the upcoming deployment. Once we received our warning order from the Pentagon, the wing began generating 24 aircraft for the deployment. This effort involved checking all the systems on the aircraft, loading wing fuel tanks and air-to-air missiles, and preparing the pilots, maintenance, and support personnel for deployment. We cancelled our day-to-day flying routine and worked around the clock for three days.

We received the execute order on the fourth day, and began processing our support people for the flight to Puerto Rico. I attended many of the prebriefs we gave our folks before putting them on leased commercial airliners. During one of the sessions, I heard the briefer tell the airmen that they needed to move their cars if they had parked in a certain area. If they were unable to move their car before they boarded the aircraft, they could expect to be towed and ticketed.

This was a helluva thing to tell our American warriors before they departed for war. I interrupted the briefer, stated that no one would be towed or ticketed, and if someone needed to move their vehicle, just let us know and we would take care of it. This statement generated a loud cheer, and embarrassed the briefer, but I told the briefer not to worry about it. I realized he was just repeating what he had been told to say by his superiors – but this was bad policy and needed to be rectified on the spot. Although it was a minor issue, it gave me an opportunity to let the airmen know their commander would take care of them, and it got the deployment off on the right foot.

The twenty four F-15s left early the next morning, and I led the first group of eight aircraft. We met up airborne with two KC-135 tankers, and flew a total of eight hours, arriving in Puerto Rico in late afternoon. Thirty minutes after we landed, the second group of eight arrived, followed by the last group of eight, thirty minutes later. Aircraft from other bases continued to arrive throughout the day, and by sunset we had our entire force bedded down.

Immediately after arriving, I met with my staff which had arrived a day earlier, and had begun standing up our operation. Fortunately, we were deployed to a U.S. Navy base with all the facilities we needed – runways, maintenance facilities, transportation, billeting, dining halls, and a full range of entertainment activities. What a way to go to war!

As I began to settle into my position as the overall commander, I held a couple of quick meetings and reviewed the latest intelligence reports along with messages from higher headquarters. The first message I read presented my first and only significant challenge. It was addressed to all the commanders in the Uphold Democracy operation and set forth certain guidelines and rules of engagement. Although most of the message was straightforward and made perfect sense, the opening paragraph created a problem from my perspective. It stated very clearly that General Order #1 was to apply to all Uphold Democracy participants.

General Order #1 was an order used during Desert Storm that essentially forbade the consumption of alcohol by all military members. At the time it was issued, it made perfect sense. We, a foreign power, were deploying to a country that did not want foreign troops on their soil and a culture that forbade alcohol consumption. However, given the extreme nature of the situation, the Saudis had invited the United States in to defend their lands and interests against Iraq.

The U.S., realizing this was a very delicate situation, felt it best to ensure there were no incidents involving drunk GI's. Indeed, we experienced very few incidents throughout Desert Shield and Desert Storm. Unfortunately, many leaders began to adopt General Order #1 as a given for any operation regardless of the circumstances. I appreciated how the order would eliminate alcohol related incidents, but I felt it was unfair to apply it across the board. An American has a right to a cold beer at the end of the workday if they so desire. It's part of our culture and always will be. There may be situations that might not allow us to indulge, but such are few and far between.

Applying General Order #1 to every operation regardless of the circumstances or the environment was a crutch for leaders who were not willing to deal with misbehavior the old fashion way – you discipline the offender, not the entire group. I appreciated, understood, and supported the necessity for General Order #1 during the Gulf War, but I was disgusted by commanders who continued to use the policy to ensure their future careers would not be jeopardized by a subordinate's misbehavior. In my mind, these were leaders who were afraid to trust their soldiers, sailors, Marines, or airmen; and, therefore, put their careers ahead of the morale and welfare of their people.

In this case, I was faced with quite a predicament. On one hand, I had received an order directing me to implement General Order #1 and forbid my airmen from drinking. On the other hand, I was faced with instituting an order I did not support, and more importantly, was unenforceable. We had deployed to a naval base in Puerto Rico that possessed all the amenities of a stateside base – officer and enlisted clubs that served alcohol, convenience stores that sold beer and wine, a base store that sold every type of alcoholic beverage imaginable and on and on. This was a far cry from deploying to a bare base in the Saudi desert where it was a criminal offense to possess or drink alcohol in the country.

Although I realized banning alcohol would possibly prevent some incidents and make my life easier, I just could not do it. Instead, I picked up the phone and called my superior at Shaw AFB in South Carolina, an Air Force three-star. I began the conversation by stating I had just read the first message from headquarters, and could not support General Order #1. First, I did not think it was necessary, and second, I could not enforce it without going to extraordinary lengths that would detract from the mission.

Fortunately for me, my boss was a true warrior leader, and quickly understood my predicament. Additionally, he had the same misgivings about General Order #1. After talking it through, he gave me permission to disregard the order with the understanding that I would be held solely accountable if there were any incidents that affected the mission or reflected poorly on the unit. I agreed.

My next action was to get the entire group together and let them know what was expected. I have always believed in getting all my people together shortly after assuming command to let them know my leadership philosophy and what I expect from them, and what they can expect from me. I felt it was critically important to do the same with this group since the majority of people had come from other organizations, and did not know me from the man in the moon.

I held the meeting in a large maintenance hangar the Navy had graciously provided for the operation. I began by talking about our mission and how important each and every individual was to its success. I also emphasized the need to work together as a team, and not as individuals with allegiance to their home base instead of this organization. All of this resonated well with the group. I ended the talk by addressing the issue of General Order #1. I stated I had been directed to implement the order, and that I had determined it was inappropriate for our situation, and that I had gained permission to disregard it. This announcement resulted in cheers throughout the hangar. I then stated I agreed to be held solely accountable for any incidents that reflected poorly on the unit or affected mission success. I added I was not concerned about accepting this risk because I knew they would not let me down. I trusted them to be ready when the time came.

Thanks to the diplomatic efforts of former President Carter and General Powell, President Clinton never ordered the invasion of Haiti. The dictatorship surrendered and left Haiti without America ever having to fire a shot. Although there was some disappointment at not being able to execute the mission after all the planning and preparation, it was overcome by the realization that none of America's sons and daughters had to be put in harm's way.

In the end, the entire deployment had gone smoothly without an incident to include any caused by alcohol. I was very proud of my team, but not surprised. During my career, airmen never let me down when they knew I trusted them, and was willing to take a risk with my personal future on their behalf.

I've found people are less inclined to screw up when they know their boss has put his trust and confidence in them. It's situations where it is very apparent the leader is only worried about his future, when the followers could care less about how their actions reflect upon their leader.

Bachelors Do Christmas Too

It was common practice in all the squadrons to schedule their bachelors for alert duty on Christmas, and such was the case with my squadron. I really did not give it much thought until one of my young lieutenant bachelors mentioned that "bachelors do Christmas too!" As I thought more about this, I realized the lieutenant had a point. At the same time,

I did not want to force my officers with families to miss Christmas morning with their loved ones. After all, one gets only so many Christmas mornings with young children, and I did not want to cause them to miss an event they could never relive. The dilemma was how to be fair to the lieutenants without causing a parent to miss an important holiday with their children.

Then it came to me. What do all fighter pilot lieutenants want to do more than anything else? Easy answer – fly, fly, fly! So why not provide an incentive for them to volunteer for alert by giving them increased opportunities to fly? My solution was to offer a weekend cross-country flight for any lieutenant who volunteered for Christmas alert duty. Problem solved. I immediately had four lieutenants volunteer for the Christmas alert.

Christmas came and was a wonderful time for all involved. The pilots with families were home with their children while the lieutenants were planning for their European flying vacation. Sure enough, as soon as January rolled around, there was a cross-country request on my desk. Being sharp lieutenants and wanting to milk this good deal for all it was worth, the pilots had requested their cross-country during a three-day weekend. They planned to depart on Friday and spend the night at a base in England known for great Friday nights at the Officers' Club. From there they were off to Madrid to spend Saturday night enjoying the Spanish night life. Sunday had them flying to Aviano Air Base in Italy with a flight to Munich on Monday for a big time in Bavaria. The cross-country mission would end with them returning to home base on Tuesday morning.

I'll have to admit, I envied the fun these young fighter pilots were going to have, but I also realized the opportunity this presented for a world-class disaster. However, a deal is a deal, so I approved the cross-country request and sent it forward to my boss, a full colonel who was the director of operations. A few days later I received a call from the colonel who had just reviewed the cross-country request.

His first question was whether or not I had actually looked at the request before I approved it. After letting him know I had, he asked if I realized the highest-ranking officer among the four was a first lieutenant. I replied that I knew and he was indeed a "damn fine lieutenant." He then asked if I understood I would be held directly responsible for any incidents that might occur. I stated I accepted the risk because I knew my guys would not let me down. He said, "fine, but do not be surprised if this backfires and cuts [my] command tour short." I appreciated his concern, but I trusted my people.

The big day finally came, and the lieutenants suited up to blast off on their great adventure. As they got ready to leave the squadron building, I thought about what I might say to send them on their way. I did not want to send them off with a threat that if they screwed up I would end their flying career, but at the same time I wanted to at least let them know I was counting on them to act professionally while still having a good time. I finally decided on just pulling them aside and expressing to them how much I appreciated their volunteering for the Christmas alert. I knew they were going to make themselves and the squadron proud during the weekend. With that, they departed on their long-anticipated great adventure.

Friday night came and went. I received a call from the command post letting me know the pilots had made it to England and their airplanes were in good shape – nothing else to report. Saturday and Sunday were the same – pilots and aircraft all in good shape with nothing significant to report. Late Monday evening I received word the pilots were safe and sound in Munich, and planning to return as scheduled the next morning. As I crawled into bed Monday evening, I felt very good about my guys and their performance.

RRRRing...... RRRRRing...... It must have been a little after midnight when the ringing of the phone broke through my deep sleep. My wife picked up the phone and passed it to me. I was still in a haze as I answered the call, but when the caller identified herself as a Grupensargent with the Munich polizei I immediately reached full consciousness. The polizei lady went on to say that she had four pilots in custody for fighting in a Gasthaus. They had listed me as their supervisor and the one to call. Now I was completely awake and pacing the floor in my underwear thinking about the great career I might have had!

As I was trying to determine how to resolve this situation, get the pilots out of jail and back to home base, she mentioned one of the pilots wanted to talk to me. However, she also stated he had a broken nose and may be difficult to understand. When the pilot got on the phone, I asked how in the world this happened. In a voice heavily laced with nasal sounds, he began to explain.

As his explanation continued, I began to hear laughter in the background and then there was a loud yell from a group of partiers – "*Got Ya!*" – and yes, they had. As it turned out, the pilots had met some young German ladies in Munich and came up with an idea of playing a joke on the boss. After sharing in their laughter, and swearing I would get even, we hung up. My wife and I slowly drifted back to sleep, laughing about it all.

The next morning, right on schedule, the four aircraft and their pilots returned without a scratch on the jets or a "real" incident to report. Of course, the word spread quickly about the prank the lieutenants had played on the boss, and how they really had me going. However, when it was all said and done, the common theme reiterated over and over again was how much the pilots appreciated me trusting them as the professionals they were.

Weeks later, when the story was being retold for the thousandth time in the bar, one of the lieutenants asked me if I ever worried about them screwing up. When I stated I really did not worry that much, he said, "Good, because there was no way we were going to let you down. When you get a commander that trusts you, that's special; and no one wants to put that kind of commander in jeopardy."

I've always remembered that, and have continued to place my trust in my people. Sure, some individuals will occasionally let you down, but, by and large, the vast majority will always work to keep a leader's trust. I believe a leader must always give trust up front – they should not require their people to earn it first. Too many leaders seem to have this backwards. They require their people to earn their trust first, without appreciating world class people deserve trust from the outset. Once your people realize they have your unconditional trust, they will do everything in their power to maintain it.

Setting the example and trusting those who depend on you are two critical aspects for leaders to internalize. When the leader sets a substantive example by exceeding their own expectations, the followers become motivated and inspired to do the same.

CREATING THE REALITY

I cannot overemphasize how important it is to have a positive attitude all the time. Your subordinates are intimately aware of your mood and disposition from the moment you enter the workplace until you depart. The manner in which you deal with people and situations quickly permeates the organization. It amazes me how often leaders are unaware of how profound of an influence they have on the organizational environment.

Rarely is there something intrinsically wonderful about the leader as an individual – there might be, but that is not the driver of subordinate behavior. The driver is often the respect subordinates feel for the position you hold. Of course they appreciate the direct influence you have on their livelihood, working environment, and progression within the organization. However, they model their behavior off you because, quite simply, you are their leader.

Some leaders never truly appreciate the impact they have on others. Something simple like a nod, a smile, or a "hello" when one of your subordinates acknowledges you in passing can have a tremendous impact. Not only do you acknowledge their presence and importance as an individual, but you can also make their day merely by recognizing them.

On the other hand, if you are so wrapped up in your own world, or worse yet, do not have the time or inclination to recognize their presence, you have demoralized and irritated your most important resource – your people. What you have just done through your act of ignoring them is send a signal that he or she is unimportant to you and, perhaps, also to the organization. Your people notice such slights, just as they notice when you make them feel special. Either approach has an impact on the way they perform. It can either be a positive or negative. The choice is yours as the leader.

If you are the type who always looks at every situation as though it is an impossible task and you have been dealt a bad hand, so will the people under your leadership. On the other hand, if you approach every situation as another opportunity to succeed and excel, your subordinates will reflect that "can do" attitude.

The Best Job in the World

As a young lieutenant, I was assigned to a pilot training squadron in Columbus, Mississippi. After I had been there a year, I was selected to become the squadron scheduler. The reason I got the job was likely because no one else wanted to be the scheduler. Well, neither did I, but my commander gave me no choice. It was a demanding job with long hours and little recognition. However, it was probably the most important job in the unit because it orchestrated the squadron's daily operations. I am convinced that being the scheduler as a lieutenant was instrumental in putting me on the road to success. How ironic it is that I did not want the position and went out of my way to avoid it! I later came to understand and appreciate how wise my commander was. He recognized the opportunities that came with this job.

The squadron was made up of eight separate flights that comprised two sections – four flights per section. The total number of pilots and students in a flight was about 25, and therefore, each section had about 100 officers attached. The flying day started early and ended late, and usually involved anywhere from 180 to 250 flying missions. It was quite a challenge to develop a schedule that met everyone's needs. Some flights had students who were pre-solo; other flights had students who were post-solo but pre-check ride; while other flights had students who needed formation or night training. Regardless of the time of year, every one of those flights had different requirements for that particular day's schedule.

As the scheduler, I worked for an officer I greatly respected and admired. At that time, I thought this major was a wise, old man. In reality, he was a young man just a few years older than me, but what set him apart from all the other officers in the squadron was his positive attitude. Regardless of the situation, no matter the time of day, he was always cool, calm, collected and positive.

It never seemed to fail – come the end of a long day, either a flight or maintenance scheduler would call with a change request that would impact the next day's schedule. These changes were usually caused by problems with the weather, a student's progress, or aircraft maintenance problems. In each and every instance, no matter how bizarre the request, this major would always respond in a very positive and professional way that every effort would be made to satisfy the request.

I was always impressed and amazed at the way in which he would handle these situations. I had observed other capable officers completely lose their composure, and become confrontational with a requester when put in a similar situation. Not that these officers were acting in an unexpected or unnatural way; I would expect most individuals to react to such bizarre requests in much the same manner. In order to satisfy the request, it usually meant that the entire schedule would have to be redone – a time-consuming and arduous task.

Therefore, it was understandable why most officers would usually respond in an argumentative and demeaning manner, with many four letter words interspersed. This type of approach certainly did not enhance a strong working relationship with other members of the squadron or the wing. On the other hand, the positive approach the major took always resulted in a strong and respectful relationship with not only other members of the squadron, but also other organizations within the wing. He became a positive force for the unit he represented by always projecting a "can do" attitude.

One late afternoon, after the entire schedule had been built, the major received one of those bizarre requests from maintenance. As usual, he responded in a positive manner and passed the request on to me. Before beginning the task, I asked him how he was able to keep his cool, and always be so positive in such frustrating circumstances. He smiled, and made me a bet that within five minutes the requester would call back and cancel the request after realizing it really wasn't doable nor helpful to the situation.

The major went on to explain why he remained so understanding and positive. First, he realized that eventually he would need help from that individual or organization. He believed it was best to keep a strong, positive working relationship with all players. Second, he had found that nine times out of ten, when a bizarre request was made, shortly thereafter it was canceled. By responding in a "can do" approach initially, both he and his organization gained great respect and gratitude from the requester. If he had responded in a negative manner, even though the request would have eventually been canceled, the requester would probably develop a low opinion of not only him, but the entire unit.

Sure enough, the phone rang a few minutes later and the caller canceled the request. The major was right on. By responding in such a positive manner, he had impressed the requester with our organization's "can do" approach and our unit had not even started work on the request. Not that there weren't times we had to change an entire schedule and work late into the evening, but usually, in those instances, the request was justified and we all pitched in to make it happen. More importantly though, his positive approach in dealing with all requests, no matter how bizarre, created a feeling of respect for our unit that was unsurpassed in the wing.

The other spin-off to his approach was that those of us who worked for him truly enjoyed our working environment, and were very proud of the reputation we enjoyed. We all adopted his positive approach in our dealings. Not only did the major influence our working environment but he also influenced our individual leadership styles.

Years later as a squadron and wing commander, I appreciated the lessons the major had taught me. There were many times when the squadron or wing received a ridiculous tasking from higher headquarters. It would have been easy to succumb to initial emotions and pursue a negative approach to the task. However, in the instance when the task was not rescinded by headquarters, and we were expected to comply, it would have been very difficult and hypocritical to then put on a positive spin in front of the airmen.

Once your subordinates have heard you ridicule the wisdom of a task, it is hard for them to understand how you can so quickly become an ardent supporter. It is much easier to start off positive and stay positive, than to move from the negative to the positive and retain your credibility.

No leader accepts every questionable tasking without challenging its merits. A responsible leader owes it to his subordinates and superiors to question a suspect tasking or request. The key is the approach the leader takes. By starting off with a positive approach, it is much easier to discuss the merits of the task versus beginning from a confrontational position. Just as I learned from the wise major, ninety percent of the time the unreasonable and bizarre tasks are quickly rescinded. And similar to my experience as a lieutenant, the organization builds an enviable and admired reputation.

Later on, in that same squadron, I had the opportunity to put a positive attitude to the test. As the squadron scheduling section leader, I had a difficult job. The section had a reputation for making numerous mistakes on the daily flying schedule. In addition, the leader I replaced was not known for his positive attitude about his job or the people who worked for him.

The section comprised about thirteen people – four pilot schedulers and nine enlisted personnel who performed much of the administrative work. We were located in a small room without any windows and four old beat up gray desks. After my first week on the job, I realized the entire section was demoralized and unhappy about being in the scheduling section. Something had to change and it was up to me to make it happen.

That weekend, I went to the local department store and bought some wood-like veneer wall paper and thirteen notebooks. On Monday morning, I brought the whole group together and told them we had a choice to make: we could either continue our poor performance or we could make a serious change. I believed we had the talent to become the top unit in the squadron and the best in the command. I admit this was a stretch, but if I didn't believe, how could I expect them to believe?

I went on to explain one of the keys to success in scheduling was attention to detail. We needed to devise some checklists to quality control our work, and processes to remember everything someone asked to do regarding the schedule. I then handed out little notebooks to every member of the section. I wanted everyone to carry them in their pocket, and when someone made a request, they were to write it down instead of trying to remember the request.

I also made the point that our work area was the pits – we needed to clean it up, and give it a professional look. Hence, the wood-like wallpaper. I planned on coming in the next weekend and apply the paper to our battered gray desks. I intended to paint the walls, put up some flying pictures, and make the office presentable. Any help would sure be appreciated if they would like to participate.

Not sure what I would find Saturday morning when I arrived at the office, I was pleased to find ten of my airmen willing to help. We spent all day cleaning, painting, and applying the wallpaper. What a difference, and the reaction from the other squadron members when they saw what we had done was encouraging. However, there was still this nagging reputation of a "mistake prone" outfit.

The next weekend I went home and made a sign. On Monday, I brought the sign into the office. It read the following:

> ### *The Aircraft Scheduling Section has gone* _____ *consecutive days without a mistake.*

As I showed each one of the section members the sign, I stated I was willing to put this sign on the entrance door to our section for all to see. Granted, we were making a bold statement about our ability to perform, and taking great risk that we would fail miserably in front of the entire squadron. This was especially risky since the section had not gone one day without a mistake in months. However, I was convinced we had the talent to back up our bravado. I was very pleased when they all agreed to put the sign up.

As soon as the sign went up, it drew a crowd with the derisive comments. I told my guys to ignore the jibes and just press on with doing their jobs. I was confident they could measure up to the task.

The first week we only were able to go two consecutive days without a mistake. The second week we went three days, but then the third week, we went the whole week without a mistake. Our confidence began to build as did our pride. The entire squadron began to pay closer attention to the sign. Some spent the whole day trying to find a mistake we might have made while others began to compliment the troops on their error-free performance.

Eventually, we achieved a record of 37 consecutive days without a mistake. When we had our higher headquarters inspection, the section was identified as the best scheduling unit in the entire command. We had come a long way, but I believed it all started with the positive attitude I displayed and how it infected all the members of the scheduling section. The best job in the world is the one you are in provided you view it that way. It is amazing how your followers will respond to your lead. If you think it is the worst, don't be surprised if they feel the same way.

As a wing commander, I had a vice commander that personified the word "positive." No matter the situation, he could always put a positive spin on our predicament. As the commander, I always appreciated his positive input into our discussions, both privately and with the staff. One of his favorite sayings was "*How hard can it be?*" He would often make such a comment after we had discussed some particular onerous task that had just been levied on the wing. Invariably, after he made the comment, all of us would begin to smile and agree that for our wing there wasn't anything too tough for us to accomplish. Then we would set to the job of getting the task done – and we would. Indeed, we created our own reality where our team could accomplish anything.

Regardless of the type of organization you lead, your attitude has a huge impact. No one wants to work for a leader with a sour, negative attitude. Yet some leaders still choose to adopt the "woe is me" and "it can't be done" attitude. If you do not believe that a task can be done, how can you possibly expect your followers to believe and then exceed expectations? It starts with the leader and the confidence the leader projects. The leader must be grounded in reality, but there is a huge gray area where reality lives. The leader who appreciates this and uses a positive approach, even in the most difficult of times, creates the belief that not only can the job be done, but can be done better than it has ever been done before.

It is commonly accepted that people are going to have bad days and to lose control now and then. However, I believe that once you accept the position of the leader, you give up the right to a have a bad day or lose control. Granted, this is a high standard, but when you meet that calling and conduct yourself accordingly, you will be amazed at what you and your followers will achieve. You should think twice before you choose to have a bad day or lose control. If you exceed the expectations of your followers, don't be surprised if they end up exceeding what you expect of them.

DECIDE TO DECIDE

I view an organization as a machine, and just like a machine the organization needs fuel to operate. Decisions are the fuel that makes an organization run. Being hesitant when making a decision is a natural human reaction since the essence of making a decision is to determine a course of action. As a leader, whenever you determine a course of action, there is a chance you may choose the wrong one.

This possibility of poor results often causes decision makers to delay decisions. Many indecisive leaders use the rationale that they need more data prior to making the decision. Although gaining data is always crucial, the reality of making decisions is that you'll never have all the information you would like. As a matter of fact, you'll be lucky to get about seventy percent of the data you desire to make the decision. The remainder will have to come from your expertise, intuition, and common sense.

This reality – that you won't have all the data and that you'll have to make up for it with your own knowledge, expertise, and common sense – paralyzes many a leader. When the leader is paralyzed, the organization becomes paralyzed and all progress ceases. It's understandable that individuals are hesitant to make a decision when the outcome is in doubt. However, the nature of leadership requires the leader to step out and make bold, clear and well-informed decisions to keep the operation moving forward.

That is not to say a leader should make decisions without any regard as to whether it will be a bad or good decision. After all, a bad decision can have just as many negative impacts as no decision. Therefore, it is imperative that the leader balances a desire for information with the organization's need for a timely decision. The leader must realize that he or she will only get a portion of the data desired to make a decision. The leader must be willing to use their best judgment, take some risk, and make the call.

30 Days

After I finished my squadron command tour in Germany, I returned to the United States and began a year's study at the National War College. Upon completion of the year, I was assigned to the Joint Staff at the Pentagon. As a branch chief in the Conventional Negotiations Division, I was involved in arms negotiations with the Russians and our European allies. I had no experience in this area, but neither did any of my fellow officers. The feeling of the military was that if you were talented enough to be promoted to full colonel, then you must possess the talents to do just about anything the military needed done. In retrospect, we managed to do a pretty good job and crafted some great agreements for our country, despite our lack of experience.

Our division was part of the Directorate of Strategic Plans and Policy led by a three-star general. Below the three-star was a two-star general and a colonel in our reporting chain. Whenever an issue came up, the proper approach was to first bring a solution to the colonel, who always had a few changes; then to the two-star general, who also had a few changes; and, finally, to the three-star for approval. On a good day, with a very hot issue, you might be able to get all the way to the three-star in 12 to 24 hours. However, most issues usually took anywhere from seven to ten days to work through the process.

Now I am not complaining about the process. As a matter of fact, I believe it worked quite well. Although frustrating at times, the process usually ensured that all options were considered and, more importantly, tapped into the knowledge our superiors possessed regarding a particular issue. For this process to work efficiently, just like any decision making process, all the leaders in the chain had to be decisive. Unfortunately, we had a weak link, and the weak link was at the worst possible point – the three-star.

On one particular occasion, an issue came to the office for an action that we had dealt with in the past. It was fairly straightforward, and none of the facts had suggested a previous decision should be changed. We were given an entire month to work the issue within the staff. Therefore, we all felt that this would be a fairly easy action to work. Such was not the case.

Our first step was to take the issue to the colonel in charge of our division. He immediately recognized it as an issue we had previously worked, and quickly approved the approach we recommended. Next stop was our two-star, who also remembered the issue, and agreed with our approach in handling it. We were making great progress. We had already cleared the colonel and the two-star in just two days. It took us two more days to get on the three-star's calendar, but we were still able to bring the issue to his attention on Day Four of our 30-day timeline.

In fairness to the three-star, he had arrived at the Pentagon a few months earlier, and was not familiar with the subject. It was no surprise that he had a few questions after hearing our presentation. We noted his questions, and committed to return with the answers. Unfortunately, the decision process did not allow us to return directly to the three-star. We were required to start at square one with the colonel.

It took a few days to answer all of the three-star's questions. We then briefed the colonel on our results, and he approved the answers and the course of action we suggested. From there, we met with the two-star and he again approved both the answers and the approach. However, by the time we were able to get back on the three-star's calendar, we were into Day Twelve.

Once again, we briefed the three-star on our recommended course of action and provided all the answers to his previous questions. After receiving the brief and the answers to the questions, the three-star presented us with another set of questions and a request for additional data. We were a little frustrated, but we still had plenty of time remaining, and appreciated the fact that the three-star was new to this business.

We returned to the office and set about getting answers to the new questions from the general. We were able to get these through the colonel and the two-star in about three days. We got back on the three-star's calendar about seven days later. We still had plenty of time left and were hoping to complete this action during the next briefing to the three-star.

After we answered the questions, and reiterated our recommended course of action, the three-star thought for a moment, and then asked us for even more data. Now we were really frustrated. Not only was this an easy issue to deal with, but we had answered every possible question the general could imagine. It was apparent to all he was asking us the same questions with a different spin, but no matter, he was a three-star, and if he desired more data prior to making a decision, we were obligated to provide it.

By now, we only had six days left to meet the suspense for a decision; still enough time, provided the three-star would make a decision. Once again, we got through the colonel and the two-star within two days. Unfortunately, the three-star was out-of-town until the day our response was due. We were scheduled to meet with him at 5:00 p.m. that afternoon.

We all sat in amazement as the general continued to agonize over making a decision on the recommended course of action. Finally, after much consternation, the three-star agreed to our approach. To those of us who had been part of this painful ordeal, this was perhaps the easiest decision we had dealt with to date. Yet, our three-star allowed himself to become so completely paralyzed over this decision, he had forced our staff to use thirty days and countless hours to arrive at the solution we had identified on Day Four.

As you can imagine, there were many other important issues we could have concentrated on during those twenty-six days. Because this officer was so concerned about making a bad decision, he frustrated his staff. By doing so, he also lost respect and credibility as our leader. Not surprisingly, the three-star retired after that assignment. I am convinced his inability to be decisive influenced his fate.

Wing King Approval

A few years later, I was assigned as commander of the 33rd Fighter Wing at Eglin Air Force Base in Florida. Shortly after I arrived, I was notified by higher headquarters to expect an inspection known as a Coronet Lightning – one of the most demanding inspections a wing could undergo. A wing was expected to receive a no-notice tasking and then prepare twelve aircraft and 500 people for deployment within the next twelve hours. The timeline was tight and success required a highly trained, tightly organized, and well led team. The clock started the minute the inspection team handed the tasking to the officer on duty at the command post. This usually occurred in the early morning hours before anyone had arrived for work. The wing was expected to recall its people, upload fuel tanks and weapons on aircraft, process individuals for deployment to a foreign country, brief the pilots, and launch the aircraft – all within twelve hours.

As the new commander, I felt it imperative to first build a strong team among my senior leaders before tackling the wing effort. I believed that one of the keys to making that team succeed was not only to ask for advice, but also to heed it. Therefore, I asked one of my senior leaders what role I should play during an upcoming exercise to prepare for the inspection. He felt the best thing I could do was to act as a "cheerleader" on the flight line while our maintenance troops readied the aircraft for deployment.

On the surface, it made sense. The most difficult part of the entire effort centered on fueling and loading weapons on the aircraft. In this leader's mind, my role as an encourager or "cheerleader" would have the greatest effect on effort. Being the new guy, I was willing to give anything a try.

We began the exercise at 3:00 a.m. one summer morning. We got off to a slow start which was expected for the first exercise. As the airmen began to get the feel of the flow, the generation started to move along smoothly. I left the flight line and went to observe the processing of the airmen we planned to deploy. After spending a little more than thirty minutes there, I proceeded to the squadron to receive the deployment brief. I was off the flight line for approximately two hours.

To my dismay, upon returning to the flight line, I found that we had ceased fueling and loading aircraft, and were beginning to defuel some of the aircraft we had already fueled. Given the short time line, there was no way we could recover the lost time and make the twelve-hour deadline.

When I investigated the cause of the problem, I was told a number of fuel tanks had nicks in them, and the maintenance personnel were unsure of their suitability for flight. When I asked who made the decision to stop the generation and defuel the jets we had fueled, I got a lot of blank stares. Apparently, no one was willing to make a decision to proceed, so the action taken was to default to the most conservative approach – stop the generation and download the tanks.

As it turned out, the nicks on the tanks were well within limits and the jets could have flown with them.

Right then, I realized that my role was not that of a "cheerleader" – I was the wing decision maker, and if the wing hoped to pass the inspection I had better be available, willing, and prepared to make decisions. For the next exercise, I put out a new policy. Only one person was empowered to stop the generation of aircraft – me, the wing commander. Anyone could make decisions to continue the generation when faced with an issue, but only one person could stop progress.

We had our next practice about three weeks later. The recall of personnel and initial response went much better. Once again, the fueling and loading of aircraft was going along according to plan. However, at the halfway point, we ran into a concern. I received a call on my radio, and immediately went to the flight line where a group of individuals were gathered around one of the aircraft.

The generation was still progressing, but there was a concern in regard to the loading of the air to air missiles. These missiles were new to the wing, and this was one of our first experiences using them during a generation. The concern was over the amount of movement in the missile after it was attached to the aircraft. It seemed to be looser than the rock solid missile it had replaced.

I asked if we had followed the technical procedures exactly as written. The answer was "absolutely."

I asked if the other missiles of this type that we had loaded were also a little loose. The answer was "yes." It seemed to me that if we had loaded all the missiles correctly, and all of them were a little loose, then that was the way they were supposed to fit on the aircraft.

It was apparent there was no one in the group, including the senior colonels, who wanted to be responsible for giving the "okay." That is to be expected. After all, these individuals were not expected to make decisions of this magnitude without gaining the wing commander's approval, and that's why I was there. I decided to press on with the generation and the flight for two reasons.

First, that is exactly the decision I would have made in a real world situation, and second, I was very confident the missiles would stay on the aircraft. Additionally, I was willing to take the risk and be held accountable if my decision was wrong.

We completed the generation within the timeline, and then flew the jets without incident. Upon checking with headquarters, we learned that the play we had experienced when loading the missiles was to be expected. This type of missile was not supposed to fit as securely as the one it replaced.

We had one more practice, and once again, another situation cropped up that required my personal intervention and decision to keep the generation going.

This practice went very well, and I was confident the wing was ready for the inspection. More importantly, so were the airmen after the great job they had done during the last two exercises.

Headquarters arrived unannounced at 2:00 a.m. one early fall morning. We recalled the wing and started the generation. Everything went as smooth as silk, and the entire operation from generation, mobilization, flight, to reconstitution turned out to be our best effort yet. The wing received the highest scores in the history of this particular inspection.

As a side note, another wing was going through a similar inspection at the exact time we were, but received a barely passing score. When pressed on the other wing's poor performance, the inspector stated the wing's senior leadership was unable to make timely decisions when faced with unfamiliar situations. This caused a breakdown throughout the entire operation.

Leaders are in place to make tough decisions, and if a leader is unwilling to address an issue, ascertain the facts, and make a timely judgment as to a course of action, the leader is of little use to the organization. There will always be risks when making decisions and as the leader, it will be up to you to assume them. When the time comes to make a decision, do not shirk from your role. Sometimes, it might require you to wait and get additional information, but more often than not, especially in critical moments, you must be decisive.

Surprisingly, followers do not necessarily expect their leaders to make timely decisions. Given a risk adverse environment that seems to be the norm, most followers expect their leaders to procrastinate, and when finally forced to make a decision, make the one with the least associated risk. It is no small wonder that followers really appreciate a leader who will gather the facts, assess the situation, and make a decision – all in a timely manner.

You see, once the leader makes a decision the followers can get on with getting the job done. What really frustrates people is the associated "down time" waiting for a decision. The leader who is willing to take the risks inherent with timely decisions will be respected by their followers. Remember, the end product is not only a leader that exceeds expectations, but also followers who do the same.

THE POWER OF EMPATHY

Empathy is one of the most important attributes a commander can bring to his or her leadership perspective. It is critical to understand and appreciate the situations your airmen and their families find themselves facing. Sometimes these situations are of their own making; however, there are times when the individual is not responsible for the difficulty they face. It is important to not confuse empathy with coddling. A leader who coddles will lose respect and be taken advantage of time after time. Empathy, properly used, can help commanders arrive at decisions that maintain good order and discipline while showing a compassionate and sincere concern for their people.

Alert Decision

I had the great fortune to serve as a commander in Europe during the height of the Cold War. Unlike the years which followed the breakup of the Soviet Union, the military, especially the one based in Europe, had a recognized threat and a clearly defined mission. In order to be able to respond at a moment's notice during this time period, we maintained a certain portion of the squadron on alert, 24 hours a day, seven days a week, 365 days a year.

Fortunately, the likelihood of an attack by the Warsaw Pact was low given a conventional attack would likely lead to a nuclear exchange and World War III. Even so, we still maintained an alert capability to demonstrate that our forces were always ready, day or night, year-round. However, as one can imagine, with a mission that had lasted for about 35 years and never been executed, complacency can easily creep into the operation. This had become the case at Bitburg Air Force Base.

Our routine was to place four fresh pilots on alert every morning at 7:00 a.m. The pilots would then serve a 24-hour tour before being replaced. If the six jets assigned to alert were all in great shape (four primary and two were spares), two of the pilots were able to fly a practice mission during their tour. If any one of the jets had a maintenance problem, the pilots would remain in the alert facility watching movies, doing paper work, or sharing exaggerated stories of previous adventures.

In addition to alert, the squadron also had many other daily demands such as flying up to twenty-four training missions, pulling flying related duties such as Supervisor of Flying, instructing newly arrived pilots, and attending numerous meetings. These other demands usually led to conflicts with the alert schedule, and we would inevitably find one of the scheduled alert pilots had a "must" meeting to attend or a training flight that conflicted with the scheduled turnover time of 7:00 a.m. The approach all three of the squadrons in the wing had begun to use was to move the changeover time around. If someone needed to fly a mission the morning they got off alert, and the brief was at 6:00 a.m. then that pilot would swap-out at 5:00 a.m. Or if there was a meeting that started at 7:00 a.m. that an ongoing alert pilot needed to attend then the swap-out would be adjusted so the pilot could make the meeting.

Although this flexible approach worked, it led to many situations where the alert force would be made up of mixtures of pilots – some from the previous day's alert force, and some from the current day. As you can imagine, senior leadership in the wing did not view this flexibility as a professional approach to our most important real world mission. This all came to a head when we received a real world scramble at 7:00 a.m. and sent out an outgoing pilot with an incoming pilot. Neither pilot had briefed with one another and both made some significant errors during the flight. After that, my boss, the Director of Operations, decreed that all squadrons would adhere to the 7:00 a.m. swap-out – no exceptions. Needless to say, we immediately made adjustments and religiously followed the guidance.

About three months after we began swap-outs at the hard time of 7:00 a.m., I got a call from one of my flight commanders. It was around 7:30 p.m., and I had just finished dinner with my family. The flight commander had just received a call from one of our new pilots who was on alert duty that night. The pilot's wife had just called him with the news that her grandmother was gravely ill, and could die within the next few days. She was upset, but wanted to know what to do about making a flight reservation and finding transportation to Frankfurt – approximately a three-hour drive from Bitburg.

The flight commander called to ask if I would approve an early change-out. This would allow the pilot to drive his wife to Frankfurt to catch a commercial flight home. All flights to the U.S. left Frankfurt at 10:00 a.m. If the pilot wasn't released, it would be a full-day before his wife could depart. I told the flight commander I would check with the DO and get a waiver. Unfortunately, the DO had just left on a trip, and I was unable to get a hold of his deputy. My wife saw and heard my frustration, and asked me what was the problem. When I passed on the circumstances, she provided a whole new perspective to this situation.

My wife had gotten to know the pilot's wife, as she always did with our new people. In the course of their conversations, the pilot's wife had shared that she had been raised by her grandmother. Her grandmother had sacrificed greatly to provide opportunities for her. She had made the most of them by graduating with top honors in high school and college. It was apparent this relationship was more of a mother/daughter relationship and this young wife was certainly experiencing deep pain and anguish. She had no one in which to turn to in her time of grief since her husband was on alert duty, and they were the only American couple in the small German town where they lived.

As I thought about this situation – a new couple to Europe, receiving such news, anxious to get back to the United States as soon as possible, wanting to support each other; yet, separated for at least another ten hours by the alert requirement – I imagined how it would be for my wife and me in a similar situation. I knew what I would want my commander to do, and so I did it. I picked up the phone and called the flight commander. I told him to call the pilot and let him know someone would be there shortly to relieve him and to get in touch with the pilot's wife to see if there was anything we could do to help in the meantime.

When the flight commander asked who would take the pilot's place I stated I was on my way to relieve him. After all, if the squadron was going to violate the DO's directive, it would have to be the commander. When I arrived at the alert facility I knew I had made the right decision. The young pilot was so appreciative I had made the decision to relieve him. It was as though the weight of the world had been lifted off his shoulders. He thanked me over and over before leaving to comfort his wife. My actions made quite an impression on the other pilots who were on alert from a sister squadron. They made a couple of comments about how impressive it was to see a commander truly put it on the line for a squadron member.

My actions allowed the pilot to get home, comfort his wife, get tickets, and get her on a flight the next day. Unfortunately, her grandmother died before she got home. Both she and her husband knew every effort was made to try to get her home in time, and that her squadron family was there for her when she needed us most.

To this day, this couple still stays in contact with us. I know how much the actions I took and risk I accepted that night meant to them. Word spread quickly through the squadron about my decision to personally replace the pilot, and it reinforced my credibility as a commander who cared as much about the people as I did about the mission.

With regard to changing out early in violation of the directive, the DO was a very reasonable man who put people first. Fortunately, he agreed with my decision and said he would have made the same call in my place. He did go on to say that this was a unique situation and he would expect me to fully comply with the alert directive in the future. I heartily agreed with his admonition.

Certainly, some will believe I erred in my actions – I can easily understand that belief. As far as violating the swap-out directive, I felt I was within my rights as a commander, with no higher authority available to waive the requirement. Whether it was justified can be argued from both sides. All I can do is explain, not justify, my rationale. For me, it was quite simple: if it were me in that predicament, I would want my commander to do what I did. Others may differ, but in the end, it is the commander who must do what he feels is right by his people, and then live with the results. A few years later, empathy came to play in another decision I made as a wing commander. Fortunately, it only involved controlling my ego rather than going against a rule.

The Red Flag

As a flying commander, I viewed leadership in the air as the cornerstone of credibility at every level. There were many commanders I served under who spent most of their time flying as a wingman vice leading the flight. The rationale given for this approach was three fold: first, commanders really do not have the time to adequately prepare for missions as the flight lead; second, because of non-flying commitments, commanders are unable to fly on a regular basis and maintain proficiency, and third, commanders can learn more about their wing's flying proficiency by observing rather than leading.

I never agreed with this rationale. I believed as a commander, you set your own priorities and should not allow your schedule to be dictated by others. Yes, this is harder to do the higher you go, but up to wing commander it is possible. A wing commander is king of his or her domain, no matter how small that may be, and certainly can manage time to allow for preparation and proficiency in the flying business. As a squadron and wing commander, I made the flying business my top priority and therefore was able to maintain my status as a flight leader throughout my tenure.

I will admit it was not easy, but I believed it was crucial for credibility with my pilots and took the time necessary to be a leader in the air. This doesn't mean I had to be the best pilot in the wing, I just had to hold my own and not embarrass myself in front of my wing. I was especially proud that I went to Red Flag (a major flying exercise) as a wing commander. I not only flew in the missions but also led as many as 24 air-to-air fighters over the deserts of Nevada. Leading large missions as a wing commander was appreciated by the young pilots, and doing so gave me a great deal of personal satisfaction. I had set as a goal to lead a large mission at Red Flag as a general officer. At that time, it had never been done. Certainly, my ego played a part in this since I knew I would be the first.

My opportunity came shortly after I pinned on my star, when the wing deployed to Nellis AFB in Nevada for two weeks. I went out with them for the first week, planning on flying four of the five flying days and leading the big mission on my last day. Everything was going perfectly. I flew the first three missions and then spent the fourth day on the ground planning for the big mission. You can imagine the surprise during the mass briefing in the auditorium when I stood to brief the plan for the sixteen ship air-to-air mission. Most of the lieutenants and captains were in disbelief that a general officer could even fly at this level, much less lead the force.

About halfway through my brief, one of my squadron commanders asked to talk to me immediately. I excused myself and went out in the hall with him. He informed me that we had just lost an F-15 on takeoff – double engine failure, and the pilot had bailed out. At Red Flag, two missions are flown every day – an AM and PM. I had been briefing while jets were taking off on the morning go. At that exact moment, I experienced my first aircraft loss as a commander.

I immediately left the Red Flag building to check on the status of the pilot. When we arrived at the scene, the aircraft was still burning. The pilot had already been picked up and rushed to the hospital. Arriving at the hospital emergency room, the first sounds I heard were my pilot's screams of agony. He was barely within the successful ejection envelope, and did not get a full chute. Additionally, he was very close to the fireball, and some of his chute caught fire, which caused him to plunge to the earth even faster. In addition to severe burns, he broke his pelvis, shoulder, elbow, jaw, and cheek. When we arrived at the hospital, he had gone into shock while experiencing the most excruciating pain of his life.

It was absolute agony to hear those screams as the doctors worked on the pilot. His injuries were so severe he was moved to a civilian hospital in Las Vegas. As we watched the ambulance drive off, my next thoughts were of his wife back at Langley AFB in Virginia. Together with the squadron commander, I went to the Nellis Command Center where an accident response team had been formed. We reviewed actions taken to date and began to put together a plan to notify the pilot's wife.

The pilot was new to the F-15 and had been married only a few years. He and his wife were full of life and a great addition to their squadron and the wing. Flying the F-15 had been his dream, and now, his dream might either kill or permanently injure him. While the team back at Langley was trying to locate his wife, I called my commander, a three-star general. He immediately inquired about the pilot's status, and then about the family – he knew there would be adequate time to determine the cause of accident, and that what was important now was the pilot and his family. When he realized the severity of the injuries, he immediately authorized an Air Force Lear jet to fly the pilot's wife to Nellis. At that time, we had not located the wife and would not for a few more hours.

Now I needed to gather the squadron together and discuss what happened. The maintenance personnel were taking this badly and felt responsible for the engine failures. Although they had absolutely nothing to do with the engine problems, maintainers have always felt a keen sense of responsibility to provide a safe, capable jet for the pilots to fly. When this does not happen, the maintainers tend to take it personally. A follow on investigation would show that maintenance played absolutely no part in this accident, but right now they were taking it hard.

After bringing everyone up to speed on the pilot's status, and letting maintenance know it was not their fault, we tackled the issue of what to do the next day. It was Friday, and there was only an AM mission planned, so it would be easy to cancel out and re-group over the weekend. I believed we needed to "get back on the horse," and we all agreed we would press ahead with tomorrow's mission. As we left the meeting, the squadron commander asked who should lead the morning mission. I stated I would, and he would be my deputy mission commander.

Returning to the command center, I found out the pilot was in critical, but stabilized condition. He was still in tremendous pain, but was no longer considered in a life-threatening situation. His wife had been located and she was in the care of a group of squadron wives, a doctor and chaplain. The plan was for her to depart early in the morning and arrive at Nellis at 9:00 a.m. After checking on a few other issues, I left for my room. During the drive to my quarters, I realized that I could not fly the mission and meet the wife when she landed since both occurred at the same time. I then began to weigh factors for why I should do one or the other. Only then did I see the "red flag of leadership" waving before me – I had to exceed my own expectations as a leader. My decision could not be about me.

The case for flying was simple: we had lost an airplane and we needed to get back into the air to regain confidence. This was a mission a commander should lead. However, I had a commander available – the squadron commander. There was no need for me to lead, other than it would allow me to achieve my goal of leading as a general officer. This was my last chance. I had just been notified that I was being reassigned to a staff job, and that meant my days of being a full time, proficient flyer were over. Never again would I have a job that would allow me to maintain my flying proficiency as I had for the last twenty-five years.

On the other hand, if my wife were flying here to come to my bedside, who would I want to greet her and assure her everything would be okay – a lieutenant colonel squadron commander or a one-star wing commander. Although I tried to tell myself it really wouldn't matter to the wife, I knew in my heart my place was with her, not in an F-15 cockpit accomplishing a personal goal.

The next morning was a sunny, cloudless day at Nellis as the Lear jet came to a stop in front of base operations. As the pilot's wife emerged, she rushed into my arms thanking me for all we had done in her time of need. I gave her a strong hug, and reassured her everything was going to be okay. As we all fought back tears, we put her into a vehicle and rushed her to the hospital to be with her husband. As she departed, flights of aircraft began taking off to fly the morning mission. The mission that would be the last opportunity I would ever have to lead a Red Flag flight.

It was a long and arduous recovery for the pilot, but one year to the day after his accident, he lifted off again in an F-15, fully recovered. The next time I saw the couple, I was speaking at a special awards banquet for their squadron. They both came up to let me know how well they were doing and that they were expecting their first child. The wife also told me that the moment she saw me out the window of the Lear jet, she knew everything was going to be okay. Not because I possessed any special healing power, but that in her mind, I represented the Air Force, and the Air Force had never let her down.

To this day, I am thankful I overcame my ego, and realized how very important the position of leadership is not only to the active duty member, but also to the family member. As a leader, there will be many instances when you will need to "walk in their shoes" or "feel their pain." When you do that, and take actions that balance the good of the institution with the well being of the individual, you will find that sometimes you will need to take risks, and other times you might need to make a personal sacrifice. But whatever the cost, I have found it to be significantly outweighed by the increased commitment to the commander and unit by the workforce and their families.

It is easy to understand why most followers would not expect a leader to empathize with their situations. From the follower's perspective, most leaders are concerned with the mission or the task and how well it is done. After all, this is what reflects on the leader. The thought that the leader would really be concerned with their personal issues, and actually engage to either resolve or mitigate them is not an expectation. Leaders who do genuinely embrace empathy will not only exceed their followers expectations but engender a commitment like no other between a leader and their people. This commitment directly translates into that desire for followers to exceed expectations because the commander did it first by leading the way with empathy.

Being Inclusive

One of the most challenging aspects of being a leader is the act of being inclusive. It is challenging because it is somewhat of an unnatural act for most people. We usually like to surround ourselves with people who resemble us, have the same beliefs, and generally choose the same approach when confronted with challenges. Although this is normal behavior for most individuals, it will create serious issues for the leader who does not adapt to a leadership style of inclusion.

Unfortunately for me, I did not fully recognize this until I had already sat in several leadership positions. Although I felt as though I was inclusive, in retrospect, I was at about the halfway point versus being fully committed to an inclusive style. This was understandable since I had spent the majority of my career flying airplanes and associating with those that either flew or maintained aircraft. I was at home with this group and would always feel comfortable working issues or socializing with flyers.

Learning from the Four-Star

Shortly after I became a one-star general officer, I was assigned to Air Force Space Command. This was done for two reasons. First, it exposed me to space operations and continued my professional development. Second, the assignment also took advantage of my expertise to help space convert from a focus on research to one more involved with operating in space. It was during this tour I learned the real meaning of being inclusive.

After I had been in Space Command for a year, we got a new boss. He was a well respected, knowledgeable four-star general who also came from the flying world. I knew him by his reputation but had never worked for him. With each passing day, I marveled at how easily he took on issues, quickly ascertained what action needed to be taken and kept all of us informed. I also noticed that he worked very hard to bring all the relevant players together when issues were to be discussed or resolved. Whenever it was decided we needed to put a team together to work a complex issue, he worked hard to identify all the players that needed to be on the team – usually coming up with three or four additional members I would have never considered or identified. He also was very patient when listening to discussions and sought out inputs from all participants.

Our previous commander had created a staff which was very effective, efficient, and productive. An extra plus was how all the senior leaders worked well together and were very supportive – something the commander fostered. So you imagine my surprise when the staff became even more productive and collegial with the new commander. The only thing

I could attribute the improvement to was our new boss's commitment to inclusiveness. Not that our previous commander was not inclusive, but our new boss took it to another level.

As I observed this behavior, I realized I had to be more inclusive in my leadership style to be as successful a leader as my boss. From that point on I began to seriously think through the requirement to be inclusive in all my dealings – professional and personal.

Whenever I put together a discussion, a conference, or a team, I would think through all that needed to be included. I began to adopt the belief "more heads are better than one" and "the more the merrier." I made sure I included those individuals or agencies that did not necessarily share my beliefs and proposed different solutions to the problem. As soon as I came up with a list of attendees, I would have my staff check it to make sure I had not overlooked someone – and in every case, I had. I recognized when all was said and done, I would get a better solution and one that had a higher probability of success.

When it came to my senior leaders, I worked hard at keeping them informed about issues, new challenges, contemplated changes and rationale for the decisions I was making. I also worked hard not to make a decision without first getting advice from my staff and subordinate commanders. I know this sounds obvious, but you would be surprised how many leaders work in a vacuum without leveraging the expertise their staff and subordinate leaders possess. From that point on, I always received feedback from my subordinates on how much they appreciated being included. Whether they agreed with my decision did not matter as much as the fact they had the opportunity to contribute.

To Clique or Not

Being inclusive as a leader involves more than just your professional life, but also a good portion of your personal life. In this area, my wife was way ahead of me, and I learned much from her example. One event that illustrates the power of being inclusive socially happened during my tour as a squadron commander. As I mentioned earlier in the book, we had taken over a group that was pretty demoralized and split up into cliques. Shortly after becoming part of the squadron, we attended our first squadron party. There were about 80 people there – husbands, wives, and bachelors. As the evening progressed, one of the popular young pilots pulled me aside and mentioned that there was going to be an "after party" at Joe's house after the formal portion of the party and my wife and I were invited.

At the conclusion of the formal party, my wife and I headed out for Joe's house. When we got there, we joined about twenty or so other squadron members. My wife and I stayed for another hour or so, and then left for home. As we were driving along I mentioned to my wife that I thought the night was a great success. She replied by telling me she thought it was an absolute disaster! Completely surprised, I questioned her as to how she could feel that way. She stated that to have an "after party" where only certain members of the squadron were included was horrible. Not only was it rude and divisive, but it was hurtful for all those couples that weren't included. "How would you like to be driving home with me tonight wondering why we were not invited?" she asked. As I thought about that and imagined some of the conversations that might have occurred between the couples not included, I agreed that the "exclusive after party" was a total bust.

The next Monday morning, I called all four subordinate commanders in and let them know that I had a problem with after parties – not necessarily having an after party but having an "exclusive" after party. Therefore, my subordinates had a choice: either we open the after party up to the whole squadron and announce the time and place during the formal party or we quit having after parties. After conferring with one another, they all agreed to continue having after parties but to include everyone.

About a month later, we had our next squadron party. Sure enough, just before we closed the event, an announcement was made that an "after party" was going to happen at Bob's place and everyone was invited. Once again, my wife and I headed for the party and we found about 30 or so people in attendance – just a few more than had attended the "exclusive" after party. However, this time the people who were not at the after party had chosen not to attend instead of being excluded from attending. I'm convinced this was a turning point for the squadron. Everyone got the message loud and clear – in this squadron, it would be one for all, and all for one. We were not going to exclude anyone at anytime; all would be included in every activity or event – it was their choice as to whether or not to participate. From that day forth we began to build a cohesive unit that would go on to become the best fighter squadron in the Air Force. We could never have done that with a fragmented unit operating with an "exclusive" approach.

Since that experience, my wife and I have always been very inclusive socially with every group we have led. When we attend any event, we make an effort to talk with every single person there. If that is difficult, then we try to spend time with those that we do not see as often to ensure we never create a perceived "favored" group of individuals. The fact is that everyone wants to have contact with the "boss," and it is important for the boss to send the signal that each and every member of the team is important and valued. It can be done by simply spending a few moments with someone sharing a story, or learning something about them. For those leaders who are naturally shy, this can be a challenging task. But, trust me, all the leader needs to do is say "hello" and the followers will take it from there. They will ask questions and keep the conversation going because, quite frankly, they like talking to the boss in a social setting away from the demands of the workplace.

This is another area where followers' expectations are easily exceeded. After all, most do not know the boss on either a professional or personal level. The thought that the leader might be interested in them from either a professional or personal aspect is not one followers often entertain. After all, the leader works and socializes in different circles. Why in the world would he or she be interested in my spouse or me?

Being inclusive, whether it is in a professional or personal setting, will always pay huge dividends. It will create a team that not only plays well together but also works well together. People will appreciate the boss valuing them and their views. Such a perspective will undoubtedly exceed the followers' expectations and ensure the leader gets the best possible advice and the most options for the challenges the organization faces. Additionally, it will create an organization committed not only to the mission but also to you, each other and, most importantly, to exceeding expectations.

ENFORCING THE STANDARDS

Standards are the expected minimum levels of quality, job performance and personal conduct required by organizations to effectively accomplish the mission. Standards can be a very powerful tool when enforced, and become little more than words on paper when neglected. As always, it is the organization's leadership that determines the level of enforcement and hence, the value added by standards.

Enforcing standards is challenging for any leader. It becomes especially difficult when dealing with the personal conduct of a workforce member, particularly when the organization's standards are higher than the accepted standards of the population at large. Such is the case with the military.

Recent incidents of extramarital affairs, sexual harassment, and substance abuse have highlighted the military's low tolerance and severe consequences for such behavior. Although this approach may seem out of step with society, there are two very strong motivators for setting higher standards of personal conduct than those required of civilian employees.

First is the overriding requirement to maintain the high level of trust we enjoy with the citizens of our nation. It is crucial for the military's very existence that the manner in which we conduct ourselves is above reproach. Why? Because we are entrusted with this nation's most precious resources – its sons and daughters. If Americans do not feel that their sons and daughters will enter a military free from harrassment and substance abuse, support for the military will vanish – and with that support, so will the funding necessary to maintain a world class organization. The public also expects those individuals who command will embody the values they deem appropriate and necessary to foster such an environment.

The military must embrace these higher standards for the good order and discipline of the force. Unlike many civilian organizations, the military is unique in its requirements and demands. First and foremost, the military expects individuals to put service above self – even when that means going in harm's way. Second, mission success is not achieved through incentives such as cash bonuses or material awards, but rather through a sense of purpose, high morale, and determination not to let fellow team members down. To recruit and maintain such a workforce, it is imperative that the environment be one of mutual respect. It is easy to see how inappropriate relationships can destroy the good order and discipline of a military organization.

The person responsible for maintaining and enforcing these higher standards is the commander. In many instances, the hardest decisions to make will revolve around these standards and the responsibility to enforce them. With my very first command opportunity at Bitburg, I almost failed that charge.

The Vanguard

This situation occurred in the mid-1980s and revolved around an incident of driving under the influence. Although it may be hard to believe now, the taboo against drunk driving is a recent addition to the accepted norms of our society. During the 1960s and 1970s, drunk driving was not necessarily encouraged, but it was certainly tolerated. However, with the toll drunk driving was taking within our society, the tide began to turn during the 1980s. Slowly but surely, what was once accepted became unacceptable and severe legal consequences followed. These consequences took the form of driver's license suspensions, heavy fines, and jail terms.

In the military, not only did we support the suspension of driving privileges and fines, we also took action to document the event in the individual's personnel folder. If the individual was in a position of responsibility, they were relieved from that position in most cases. Such events are usually career-enders.

As I mentioned earlier, in the beginning of my career, drunk driving was not encouraged, but certainly tolerated. It was not uncommon for many of the attendees at a squadron party to drive home under the influence – some in better shape than others, but nevertheless, not in any condition to drive.

As we made this transition from an environment of toleration to zero tolerance, it was difficult for everyone. Initially, we ignored it. Then when several individuals were caught and punished, we began to come up with mitigators – taxis, designated drivers, *etc*. I was fortunate my wife usually watched after me and drove home; however, there were times as a young officer when I threw caution and good judgment to the wind and acted irresponsibly. During this early time in my career, the issue never created difficulties for me. I had not reached the command level yet, and I was only responsible for my own behavior. That all changed about six months into my first command.

I had just arrived at the squadron when my executive officer greeted me with news that one of our squadron pilots had been arrested the day prior for drunk driving. The officer was one of the senior leaders in the squadron. He was a strong pilot and everyone liked him. He wasn't a super star, but he was a solid citizen with an above-average record.

I felt sorrow and empathy for my officer. After all, if it were not for the grace of God, there go I! It was at this point I made my mistake. I determined my role as the squadron commander was to somehow get this officer off with no significant punishment. After all, he did what so many had been doing for years and were still doing. Unfortunately for him, he got caught. Any type of formal punishment would find its way into his record and ruin his chances for further promotion and command. I was convinced my role as commander was to protect my guy even though he was guilty as charged.

Shortly thereafter I received a call from the base lawyer who was responsible for the administrative handling of the case. In the military, lawyers are advisers to the commanders. They have no role in determining the charges brought against an individual or determination of punishment – that is the role of the commander. However, the lawyers advise commanders on precedent and what the Air Force views as appropriate punishment. Still, it is the commander who ultimately makes the decision and administers punishment.

As soon as I talked to the lawyer, I knew I had problems. The Air Force had become very strict with drunk driving and expected an offender would receive formal punishment involving documentation in their personnel folder, a fine, and loss of driving privileges. Realizing this was a death knell for this officer, I countered with an offer to verbally counsel the individual and "really chew him out." The lawyer stated this probably would not be acceptable, but he would pass my proposal on to the wing commander. I knew this would be a tough fight, I felt good about two things. One, I was trying to protect my guy, and, second, the approach had been forwarded to the wing commander and I was sure he would support me. I was wrong on both counts.

My wing commander was a fighter pilot's fighter pilot and an individual for whom I still have great respect to this day. Knowing he would feel the same empathy I felt, I was confident he would support my approach. When I received a call that he wanted to discuss the case with me, I was a little surprised but thought he might want to give me some words to use in my verbal counseling session.

Fortunately for me and my future command opportunities, the wing commander not only disagreed with my approach but took the time to explain why. First and foremost, he stated:

> *You've got your loyalties mixed up. You think your loyalties belong to your airmen regardless of circumstances. That is wrong – your airmen demand your loyalty and support as long as they are adhering to the standards, rules, and expectations the Air Force has set for them. Your first and overriding loyalty is to the institution that has placed you in command. When you receive command, you are expected to embrace, exemplify, and enforce the standards of the institution. If you can't do that, then you should not accept command. If the institution cannot count on its leaders to enforce the standards, then who will? The answer is no one, and the standards become little more than words on paper. As a leader, you have obligations to your people who go astray. However, your obligations are tied to ensuring people are treated fairly and receive proper coun-*

sel, and when there is a range of punishment, the person's prior performance and future potential is considered. Your role is not to protect individuals who have fallen short of standards. Otherwise, those standards will slowly but surely erode until they have no influence whatsoever on the institution.

At first I was deeply upset over the wing commander's counsel, and initially chalked it up to the fact he had lost his bearings. However, the more I thought about his admonishment, I began to appreciate the wisdom of his counsel. It is true – leaders are the vanguards of the standards. If leaders do not embrace and enforce the standards, the standards have little impact on the workforce and hence, the institution. There is nothing worse than setting high standards and then lacking the moral courage to enforce them. It makes a mockery of the standard and takes credibility away from the institution it supposedly supports.

Enforcing the standards is not easy. It's likely the hardest job a commander might face. The reason is simple – enforcing standards of behavior will occasionally force a boss to do *bad* things to *good people* who have done *bad* things. It is much easier to do bad things to bad people who have done bad things. Additionally, these actions will usually have difficult consequences for innocent family members who had nothing to do with the transgression. Regardless, for the good of the institution, one must be able and willing to not only adhere, but also enforce the standards of the organization.

The Love Bug

My most graphic example of the need to enforce standards occurred during the time I commanded the 1st Fighter Wing and took a contingent of 1,500 people to the desert of Jordan for three months. This deployment took place in the mid-1990s when the Air Force was transitioning from an overseas-based force to a CONUS-based deployable force, and this was the concept's first complete test. It generated a great deal of interest throughout the Air Force and the defense establishment. The expeditionary wing, as it was called, involved aircraft and personnel from four stateside wings. My wing at Langley provided the bulk of both personnel and senior leadership.

As I prepared for this deployment, I realized it would be significantly different from others I had experienced. We were deploying to a country that had little involvement in the past with U.S. forces. We also would be living in a tent city with the barest of conveniences for three months. And finally, the wing would be composed of about 1,350 men and 150 women.

Jordan was a unique country in the Middle-East. Although small without much material wealth, it had played a significant role in many peace negotiations brokered by the United States. Unfortunately, Jordan's alliance with Iraq during the first Gulf War caused some strained relations between Jordan and the U.S., so there was a spirited effort to make this a successful deployment and lay the ground work for a new start. It was imperative that the airmen performed in an exemplary manner, and did not create an embarrassing situation for either government.

In addition to this being a high stakes diplomatic deployment, it was also seen as the new template into which the USAF would transform to meet the challenges of the 21st Century. Several senior general officers and civilian leaders expected a near flawless deployment to set the stage for an Air Force based on an expeditionary concept. Thrown into this equation was the fact we would be deployed in the middle of the desert, in a very different culture, and live in tents with the few conveniences and distractions. Finally, with both men and women deploying together as a single force, any commander could immediately realize the potential for a new set of challenges.

When men and women are put together in the middle of the desert with little to do during their free time – *watch out!* I knew the only way to prevent the possibility of the deployment turning into a Love Boat episode was to address the issue immediately, and demand that all personnel abide by Air Force standards.

Women have been part of our military since its beginning. But it wasn't until the 1970s that women began to join the military in record numbers. Since then, women have become an integral part of our military and are critical to accomplishing the mission. As of 2009, women make up sixteen percent of the force and almost all career fields are open to them. They are represented in every rank from Airman Basic to General and they are vital to each of the armed services.

With this transition into every aspect of military life, there has been a cultural change within the services. No longer is it acceptable to consider the military a "man's domain." The services don't tolerate discrimination, harassment, or inappropriate relationships within the ranks. I don't mean to suggest this type of inappropriate behavior doesn't occur, but when it does, senior leadership is expected to take corrective action to deal with the infraction.

As a commander, I have always found it to be very helpful to meet with my people as soon as I took command. This allowed me to convey my vision and philosophy for the unit, and it put a face with a name for the airmen. Additionally, it allowed me to reinforce the standards I was charged to uphold. I had done this since my first command, and found it to be beneficial no matter the size or composition of the organization.

The fact I was commanding a unit composed of four different organizations, based in a foreign country, and experimenting with a new concept with high expectations for success, demanded I get the airmen together and set the tone. That is exactly what I did with three different sessions on the second day in country. My talk primarily revolved around the importance of the mission and the great opportunity each of us had to participate in this historic undertaking, and the need for us to work together as a team to ensure success.

At the end of my talk, I laid out my expectations for each individual's behavior during the deployment. I specifically addressed the need to respect the Jordanians and their culture, and the importance of respecting one another. I reiterated the Air Force's standards with regard to relationships between the sexes. Quite simply, I stated that if you are married you should act married, Now was not the time to have a mid-life crisis and see whether or not you still might be attractive to the opposite sex. Second, if you're single and attracted to another single member, get their phone number and get together when you get back to the States. But for now, concentrate on your job and your responsibilities. I added that any violation of these standards would result in swift and harsh punishment.

There are some who might feel it was unnecessary to discuss behavioral standards between the sexes. After all, what goes on between two people is their business, as long as it is done discreetly and does not affect job performance. My point was that any type of sexual relationship in a deployment setting would not remain discreet and would likely affect job performance. It's very important to address the issue up front, set the standard, and present the consequences for failure to adhere to expectations. If the leader waits to address the issue until there is a known transgression, the "love bug" will be running rampant through the organization. It will be impossible to get the genie back in the bottle.

So there is no misunderstanding, I did not do this because I was on a moral crusade. My sole motivation was ensuring the success of the deployment. If individuals wanted to enter into questionable relationships that was their business and they would bear the consequences. However, when those relationships affected the success of the deployment, then that was my business. Having been around a few years, I knew that any sort of sexual relationship would negatively affect the deployment. Individuals would become more concerned about their "new love" than doing their job. Such relationships, especially between officer and enlisted, could lead to speculation of preferential treatment for the lower ranking member. All in all, nothing good would come out of a deployment romance.

The first week of the deployment, everything was working smoothly and the operation was coming together nicely. At night, we would gather in a secluded area away from the Jordanians, enjoy a few beers (limited to three for obvious reasons) and listen to music. One night it would be soul, then rock, country, and so forth. It was a great opportunity to relax and bond together as a professional team. As the night would wear on some of our folks would dance. But realizing I was there along with other senior leaders, and knowing the standards, the dancing never degenerated into anything racy. I am convinced if I had not set the standard early that exact behavior would have started.

During the third week, one of my commanders came to me with the report that a couple had been caught the night prior having sex. Even though I had made the standard clear, I had not organized a sex police to enforce the policy. Senior leadership was expected to monitor the environment and if they saw something out of place they would address it. In this particular case, our security forces were making a routine patrol when they heard unmistakable sounds coming from a supply tent. When they investigated, they caught the couple "in the act."

These situations are never easy. The man was a young single airman, but the woman was a newly married lady. Both were from different bases, but worked in the same section during the deployment. The woman's husband was also in the military stationed at their home base. I was unhappy about the situation, especially since I knew any punishment of the woman would result in her husband finding out the circumstances. I didn't know how this might affect their marriage, but I could imagine how it would affect mine if I were in that predicament.

Regardless, standards are standards, and unless they are enforced they are meaningless. By noon, word had passed through tent city that a couple had been caught having sex. There was no doubt in my mind the airmen were wondering about what action would be taken. My decision was quick – both individuals were to be sent home the next day and formally punished. Additionally, I placed an article in the local paper we had created to keep the airmen informed. It was short and to the point. The article stated the security forces caught a couple in a compromising situation, and they both had been sent back to their stateside units with a formal reprimand and a hefty fine. The airmen knew this disciplinary action was probably a career-ender for both. When the word got out the woman was married, it certainly gave all married personnel cause to reflect on whether a deployment fling was worth the consequences.

That was the only incident we had during the three-month deployment. Now I am not naïve enough to think that was the only incident – it was the only incident that I knew about. I am sure some of my more determined risk-takers found a way. However, I had created an environment during the deployment that deterred such behavior, and led to a deployment more focused on mission accomplishment. I would have hated to work through all the situations that could have developed if I had not set and enforced the standard from the beginning. I learned my lesson early about the need for leadership to accept the responsibility for standards and to appreciate the role they played in an organization's success or failure.

In the latter stages of my career when I would mentor new commanders, I would discuss the importance of standards and the commander's role. I would ask them to envision the Chief of Staff and the Secretary of the Air Force trying to determine who should lead their unit. In the end, they both settled on this officer because they trusted he/she had the courage to enforce the standards of the Air Force. By enforcing those standards, the Air Force would remain the world-class organization that it is today. I hoped by creating such a scene in the minds of new commanders they would appreciate the magnitude of their responsibility and the loyalties incurred. The overall deployment was an absolute success and laid the foundation for the Air Force's eventual transformation to an expeditionary force.

The military takes a different approach to standards because of its culture. However, that is not to say that the private sector does not have a requirement for standards or a need for leaders to enforce those standards. Organizations that do not set high standards for the quality of their product, or the integrity and behavior of their people will lose market share and business. Just as in the military, it is up to the leadership within the organization to maintain and enforce the standards. Without that enforcement, standards are just meaningless words on paper.

People expect their leaders to enforce the standards. Standards and integrity are areas where the followers do have high expectations and failure to meet them have severe negative consequences for the leader and the organization. Leaders must understand there is little wiggle room when enforcing standards of behavior – a person either met them or did not. When imposing punishment on someone who is guilty of violating a standard is where a leader has some discretion. Still, gross violations are expected to be met with harsh consequences.

One area a leader must be absolutely pure is in the application of the standards and the consequences imposed. Clearly stated, standards apply to all personnel regardless of position or stature. Unfortunately, some leaders allow personal relationships or a person's position to influence their actions when faced with the need to enforce a standard. When the leader lacks the courage to do the right thing, he/she seriously falls short of follower expectations. Although the followers may appreciate the difficult situation the leader is in, they nevertheless expect a proper application of the standard.

Unfortunately, followers are not that surprised when a leader fails to meet their high expectations. They just chalk it up to the cynical "*it's a who you know that counts*" mentality. Leaders who consistently apply standards equally and fairly, regardless of who may be at fault, will always exceed expectations.

Integrity

Integrity makes up a leader's inner soul. It is the compass by which leaders guide all their activities – both personal and professional. When a leader proves to be untrustworthy, the leader loses the moral authority necessary for success in command. Granted, individuals without an ounce of integrity have been successful, but they never capture and maintain their followers' respect or commitment. And without that respect and commitment, a leader will never be able to take an organization to extraordinary levels of achievement. My experience has shown that a lack of integrity always catches up with a person no matter who they are or what position they've achieved.

Being human, most of us have fallen victim to the temptation to lie or cheat. Granted, most of our transgressions occurred when we were young and revolved around cheating on schoolwork, and/or lying to our parents – offenses which have been committed by every generation. The critical issue is when the lying and cheating stopped and when the building of a personal integrity base began.

For me that happened the day I raised my hand and became a cadet at the Air Force Academy. For others it may have also been at a similar age, but regardless, at one point or another, most of us had to make the choice to become and act as an honorable person. It is an easy choice to make, but a hard one to keep. After all, almost all individuals would like to be honorable, but not all individuals are willing to pay the price required – humankind has been deceiving and lying to one another since the very beginning.

Integrity is critical for a leader because successful leadership requires followers to place their trust in their leader. When they are able to do that, most followers willingly place all of their talents and energy at the disposal of the leader. It is when the leader's integrity is in question that followers tend to hold back or only halfheartedly commit themselves to the task. An organization that expects to exceed expectations can only do so with a leader of rock solid integrity.

Shine Your A**

The first time I really had an integrity challenge was when I was a lieutenant as an instructor pilot. I was assigned to a pilot training wing at Columbus Air Force Base in Mississippi instructing in the T-38. I loved my job, and looked forward to work every day where I would fly at least twice if not three times, weather permitting. As a new instructor, I was assigned to an experienced instructor who helped teach me the ropes and guide me through the pitfalls of flying with students. Near the end of our six-month training period, we went on a weekend cross-country flight.

After we had gassed up at our first fuel stop, we climbed back in the jet, started her up, and taxied out for take-off. When we got to the take-off position, my buddy instructor pilot took control of the airplane and stated he would demo how to take-off when on a cross-country weekend. What ensued was essentially a "shining your a**" maneuver. After the jet lifted off the runway, the pilot raised the gear and leveled the jet at about 50 feet, then accelerated to about 300 to 350 knots in afterburner, and at the end of the runway abruptly pulled the nose up into a 30-45 degree climb that usually topped out at 5,000 feet. For the casual observer on the ground it was an impressive display, and for the pilot it was an outlet from the tedium of teaching students day after day. Needless to say, this was not a sanctioned Air Force T-38 take-off procedure and was only done at bases away from home base and bases not in the training command.

Now that I had completed my check-out cross-country flight, I was cleared to fly with students on cross-country missions. I immediately signed up for a cross country, and was scheduled for the following weekend. We took off as scheduled on Friday morning and headed for our first stop. After we refueled and were taxing out, I took control of the airplane and flew my first non-standard take-off. It was exhilarating, fun, and made me feel like I was really a hot shot.

We flew to five or six different bases on that cross-country and I did one or two more non-standard take-offs. Our final flight back to Columbus originated from Shaw AFB. We planned to take-off late so as to get a night training sortie. After three days of constant flying and partying, both the student and I were ready to get home. As we taxied out I had already decided to let the student make the take-off and relax on the way home. However, just as we were cleared for take-off, a young airman who checked over our jet at the end of the runway motioned for me to make a non-standard take-off. A surge of adrenalin poured through me as I realized I had a chance to impress someone with my flying skill. I took control of the aircraft and made the take-off. Once I leveled the aircraft off, I gave control back to the student and we continued on to Columbus for landing.

As we entered the squadron after landing I noticed the operations officer was still there. This seemed a little odd since flying was completed and the squadron was just about deserted save a few instructors and students. As I was hanging up my parachute, the ops officer asked if he could see me in his office. This also was odd since I didn't have that much interaction with the ops officer as a new lieutenant instructor pilot.

You can imagine my surprise and then shock when the first words out of his mouth were "I need to read you your rights!" After the surprise and shock wore off, I responded that I knew my rights and would be happy to answer any questions. The first question was "what kind of take-off did you make when you left Shaw AFB?" From his tone, I quickly realized I was in serious trouble and that my whole future was at risk. My dream of becoming a jet pilot, realized only two years earlier, was in serious jeopardy. As these thoughts went through my head so did the idea that maybe I should lie or at least quibble with my response. After all, this was my future, and there was nothing more important to me at that time than flying airplanes. To give it up was a fate worse than death and possibly a justification for a lie that might save me.

Fortunately, I did not consider lying as an option very long, and admitted to my ops officer that I had indeed flown a non-standard take-off that was not according to procedures. He then had my student and me make written statements, and told me to report to the squadron commander in service dress uniform first thing the next morning. There would be no need to wear my flight suit since I was grounded until this matter was cleared up. As I drove home that night, my world was at an end. My wife tried to console me, but I spent the night wide-awake and in utter despair.

The next morning I arrived at the squadron bright and early and reported to the squadron commander. The commander was a career fighter pilot who had spent almost six years as a prisoner of war during the Vietnam War. I did not know him very well, but he had always been very cordial to me and I had great respect for him.

After returning my salute, he asked me in a serious but friendly manner what had happened at Shaw. I stated I had made a non-standard take-off, and then described it to him. Being a fighter pilot who had probably flown more non-standard maneuvers than I would ever know, he sort of smiled after I described what I did. He then stated that those guys at Shaw wouldn't know a real "shine your a**" maneuver if they saw one. He told me to go on back to my flight room, and he would try to clear up this incident.

Based on my initial discussion with my commander I felt relieved. I knew I was still in trouble, but at least I did not feel I would be cashiered out of the Air Force and lose my wings. About an hour after this discussion, I was called back to the squadron commander's office. As I entered his office, I could tell that his mood had changed considerably from when I had left. This time he kept me standing, and he looked at me with a very strained and fierce look. Then he said very slowly, "OK, Looney, I'm going to give you one more chance to tell me exactly what happened at Shaw. And I mean exactly what happened with that take-off and exactly how you flew it!"

Although I was extremely nervous and uncomfortable, I once again recounted how I made the take-off – how high I leveled off above the runway, how fast I got, how nose high I pulled the aircraft, and the altitude I leveled off. When I finished, he gave me a cold stare and then said, "Think real hard, because I am only going to give you this one chance to set the record straight." I responded that there was no need to change what I said since that was exactly what happened.

Then the commander walked behind his desk and stated, "I just got off the phone with the Shaw Director of Operations (a full colonel), and he said you held the airplane off the runway at five feet, you accelerated to 500 knots, you went past the runway, overflew a road and caused a car to veer off, and then you pulled the nose straight up and did aileron rolls through 10,000 feet."

When the commander finished, I stepped forward, slammed my fist on his desk and said loudly, "Sir, that's a lie!" I could tell that I had caught him entirely by surprise with my actions – as a matter of fact, I surprised myself, but what I was being accused of was so inaccurate it set me off. As I regained my composure, I could tell my outburst had impressed him since it was obvious it was a sincere reaction to the untrue accusation. I believe this act on my part convinced my commander I was telling the truth. He began to smile and stated that he believed me but he had to make sure. Although the Shaw DO had reported the incident this way, he believed my version, and now even more so based on my reaction. Once again, he told me to return to my flight room and await further directions.

As I sat alone awaiting my fate, the discussion of the day among the IPs was my take-off and present situation. Interestingly enough, there were a number of officers who questioned whether I should have admitted to making the nonstandard take-off. In my mind, there was no question that I should acknowledge my breaking of the rules and take my punishment. Others thought it would be difficult to prove, and given that my flying career was at stake, perhaps it was worth lying about. Although their comments did not increase my confidence in my actions, inside I knew I had done the right thing, and I would let the chips fall where they may.

While I was stewing in my flight room, significant discussions were being held between my commander and Director of Operations (DO). To this day, I owe my career to the reasoned and fair approach these two men took in dealing with this situation. Appreciating that there was a significant difference between my story and Shaw's version, the DO realized he did not have enough data to make a decision on what really occurred and what action to take. After all, one was a minor violation of rules, while the other was a major violation being covered up by a lie. Fortunately for me, the DO was determined to know the truth before he took any action.

He called in two of his most experienced T-38 instructor pilots and sent them to Shaw in a T-38. Once there, they performed three take-offs for a group of individuals who witnessed my take-off. One take-off was done according to procedures, another one done the way I described, and the third one attempted to mirror the Shaw version. The Shaw version was difficult to replicate because the airplane did not have the power to perform in that manner. This effort took three days, and I nervously awaited their return. I was confident I would be vindicated, but there's always that chance that things might not turn out as expected.

After they flew the last take-off, the instructors conferred with the Shaw contingent to determine which profile most replicated my take-off. Thankfully, all of the witnesses picked the one I had described and flown. The Shaw DO had not witnessed my take-off, and had gone on hearsay as to what type of maneuver I had flown. After getting the results from the instructors, the DO called my commander and passed the news to him. Late that afternoon, my commander called me into his office.

As I sat down, he told me to relax, the ordeal was over. I had been proven innocent of the Shaw charge but was guilty of a minor violation. My DO felt I had been punished enough – grounded for a week along with the professional embarrassment and thus, cleared me to go back to flying. The commander also passed on that both he and the DO appreciated my honesty and willingness to admit my transgression. Earlier, two other instructors violated regulations and had tried to lie their way out, but were caught. These two individuals were no longer flying airplanes, and their careers were essentially over. My commander stated I would have suffered the same fate if I had chosen to lie.

This was my first experience where I had the option of trying to deceive to protect my future, or admit to a mistake and take what might come. During my time at the Academy, I had never been placed in such a position, so I never truly had to test my commitment to being an honorable person. The lesson I learned from this experience has stayed with me.

Granted, I was extremely fortunate to have had such a wise DO. He could have very easily accepted the Shaw version and hammered me. He was under no obligation to determine the facts to the level he did. Thankfully for me, that was the approach he took. To this day, I think of him and his approach whenever I am faced with a similar situation. And just like him, I am appreciative of the individual who tells the truth and give no quarter to the one that lies.

As I progressed through the ranks and assumed more command positions, I appreciated the need for integrity in all dealings. Not just when one screws up and is caught but in every dealing we have with our subordinates and our superiors. Trust is crucial in any organization and it starts at the lowest level. Subordinates must believe their superiors have both their individual best interests as well as the organization's as the top priority. Superiors must know that their subordinates are reporting correctly on the status of their organizations, operations, and responsibilities. When this doesn't happen, the results can be disastrous.

SORTS Reports

Shortly after I assumed command of the 1st Fighter Wing, I quickly realized that the constant deployments to Southwest Asia were taking a toll on my people and their equipment. We had three F-15 fighter squadrons and two of them were deployed to the desert at least six months out of every year. This operations tempo put a tremendous strain on our airmen, their families, and our equipment. Additionally, it was a different operations tempo than the one we had for the past fifty years.

During the Cold War, our nation followed a strategy called forward presence that required the stationing of forces around the world. The concept relied on those forces to face the initial attacks of an enemy while reinforcements flowed from the States to enter the fray. With the end of the Cold War, this strategy was no longer viable or affordable and our nation significantly reduced our presence overseas. However, situations in the Persian Gulf and Balkans required a constant U.S. military presence, so our air forces found themselves in a constant stream of 90 to 120 day rotations to these hot spots.

Prior to these constant deployments overseas, our Air Force had enjoyed relative stability during the Cold War years. We moved from stateside to overseas bases with three-year tours being the norm. Additionally, during the 1980s, the military enjoyed a significant plus up in funding that resulted in new equipment and plenty of spare parts. Very seldom during this period were any of our units short of equipment, people, parts, or money – it was a unique period for our military, and it was reflected in our operational readiness reports.

Standardized Operational, Resource, and Training Status (or SORTS) is the vehicle the U.S. military used to report readiness to the National Command Authorities. In the case of the Air Force, each squadron in an operational wing reported their readiness status on a monthly basis. The ratings ranged from C1 to C5, with C1 being the highest state of readiness. These ratings were determined by an objective measurement of a unit's personnel, equipment, and training status. A subjective commander's assessment was included that could either upgrade or downgrade the rating based on circumstances. During the 1980s and early 1990s, it was unusual to have a unit report less than C1. After all, the Air Force was enjoying an abundance of people, equipment, parts, and superb training opportunities. This all began to change during the 1990s.

With funding cutbacks and force reductions, all the services found it more difficult to maintain readiness levels. As the years passed, and more people were cut from the roles of the military, fewer parts were purchased, and more deployments were added to the schedule, the predictable, stable environment the Air Force once knew transformed into one of high intensity, ambiguity, and underfunding. This put commanders in uncharted territories because now some of the units did not possess the required number of people, equipment, or training levels to meet C1 criteria. Unfortunately, some commanders opted to use their assessment discretion to call their units C1 when it was really a stretch.

The reason for these inflated ratings falls into basic human psychology. We are all taught to put our best foot forward and always find a way to make it happen. Individuals who whine and constantly bemoan their personal predicament are quickly written off as "losers." Although this attitude has allowed extraordinary accomplishments by individuals or units when the odds are against success, it also can create an environment where commanders are more interested in looking "good in the shower" versus "telling it like it is."

This is what happened in the late 1990s. Air Force units had enjoyed high readiness rates for years and commanders were reluctant to state their organization was either unable or severely constrained in accomplishing their wartime mission. When I became 1st Fighter Wing commander all three squadrons were rated as C1, when in my opinion only one was truly C1, with another being C2, and the third C3. The cause for this was quite simple – personnel shortages, unplanned high operations tempo and parts shortages. In order to get one squadron C1 to deploy to the desert, we found we had to take people, equipment, and parts from the other two to "make it happen." Yet, every month we continued to send forward reports that stated all was well at the 1st Fighter Wing.

During my first wing readiness brief, I stated we needed to change our approach for two reasons. First, it was imperative that we state our true status to our military and civilian leadership – after all, they were making decisions about military responses to world events based on our readiness reports. Second, if we ever hoped to improve our readiness through increased funding and additional people and parts, we had to let our leadership know we were hurting.

Although both those reasons seem obvious, it was very difficult for Type-A, over-achieving commanders to state if their unit was broken. However, I was determined to provide accurate reports, and I pressed commanders to justify ratings that were inflated in my opinion. By the end of my third month in command, I finally got ratings reflecting our unit's true status.

During this time, a hurricane approached Langley and we implemented a plan that required us to fly our aircraft off station, button down the base, and evacuate families in low lying areas. I was very pleased with the performance of the wing during this event, and even more so since not only was the 1st Fighter Wing based at Langley, but so was Headquarters Air Combat Command (ACC).

ACC was commanded by a four-star general who was responsible for the vast majority of fighter and bomber aircraft in our Air Force. Although he was not my direct boss, there was no doubt in my mind who the real boss at Langley Air Force Base was – and it wasn't me! Therefore, I had kept the four-star updated on all our actions leading up to and during the hurricane. It was at my final update after the hurricane had passed that I realized how important it is for commanders to always tell it like it is.

After my update, the ACC commander casually asked if I had received the tasking order to prepare two of my F-15 squadrons for immediate deployment to Southwest Asia. Saddam had once again made provocative moves towards Saudi Arabia and the U.S. was preparing a military response. I stated that I had not received the tasking and was surprised two squadrons were being tasked since I only had the ability to send one. I could tell by the commander's body language this caught him by complete surprise.

"What do you mean you have only one squadron available? I'm positive my staff told me your guys were ready to go with two squadrons."

"Sir, I'm not sure what your staff passed to you," I replied, "but I do know that my SORTS report states that I have only one squadron available."

With a perplexed look, the four-star picked up the phone and asked for his Director of Operations (DO) to report to his office. The DO was out of town, so the assistant, a colonel, quickly reported in. In a very calm and deliberate voice, the four-star asked if headquarters had tasked the 1st FW to send two F-15 squadrons to the desert as he had been briefed. The colonel quickly stated that when the staff went back to draft the message tasking the 1st per his direction, they realized our SORTS report allowed us only to send one. Therefore, the staff ordered the 1st and the 33rd to each send a squadron in order to meet the tasking. The colonel stated the change had just been made and the tasking was about to be sent out to the wings.

Silently I breathed a sigh of relief. I could only imagine what would have happened if my SORTS report had not reflected our true capability and we would have been tasked to send two squadrons. My only recourse would have been to acknowledge that my SORTS report was misleading and the wing did not truly possess the capability I had reported to my commander. Not something I would have enjoyed doing, and certainly would have reflected poorly on my judgment, professionalism, and integrity.

As it was, the ACC commander shrugged and said he understood and asked if I would have any trouble making that tasking since my jets had been evacuated for the hurricane and were not due back to Langley until the next day. I stated that as long as I had them back by tomorrow, we could meet the tasking. With that, he stated he was happy with our response to the hurricane and had every confidence we could generate and deploy to Southwest Asia as expected.

I smiled, saluted, and left his office with the colonel. As I drove back to my office, I reflected on how differently I would feel if events had gone the other way. It would have been easy to upgrade all my squadrons SORTS status to reflect a top rating, but it would not have been true. And although it would have looked good on paper, the false rating would have blown up in my face. To me, this was just another reinforcement of how important it is to tell the truth.

Too often individuals feel it will reflect poorly on their status as a leader if they raise warning signs to their leaders. In their minds, it is better to keep bad news to themselves, and hope it never sees the light of day, versus taking the chance they may be perceived as a whiner. Granted, if you are always saying the sky is falling, and your efforts to resolve your challenges are half-hearted, your boss may see that as an indication of poor leadership skills. But, on the other hand, if circumstances beyond your control prevent you and your organization from being able to perform your mission, you are duty and honor bound to inform your leadership so they can help solve the problems. Telling them your accurate status when it is showtime is too late, and sets not only your organization up for failure, but also the leaders and organizations above you.

Integrity applies across all walks of life and to all individuals. For leaders, it is even more critical because decisions that affect the welfare of the organization and workforce are made on a leader's input. As a leader, a lack of integrity will not only result in disaster for you, but may well bring down your entire organization and many innocent workers.

Followers expect their leaders to be pure when it comes to integrity. In some cases, followers will be betting their lives on the leader's commands. There is an absolute demand for the highest level of honesty. When leaders fail to meet this expectation, they lose the trust and confidence crucial to organizational performance. These transgressions from the standard need not be gross. Tendencies to waffle and obscure can be just as damning as outright lies and deceptions. The follower needs to know that his or her trust will not be violated by the leader. Any action by the leader which causes followers to doubt their leader's integrity is *fatal*. When it comes to integrity, the *standard has to be perfection*.

PROFESSIONAL COURAGE

—⊷⧜⊷—

As a leader, one of the most difficult demands of the job is to fire a subordinate who is not making the grade. Like most other individuals, I find it difficult to inflict pain and suffering on another person. Granted, when the individual knowingly lies, cheats, deceives, or breaks the rules it is a little easier. However, even in these cases, there are usually innocent family members that are caught up in the mess, and hurt by the punishment inflicted on the perpetrator.

By far, the most difficult situation occurs when an individual has done nothing wrong but for whatever reason is not suitable for the position. The hardest thing I have ever done is tell someone who had done their very best that their best was not good enough. Every leader must be willing to do this for the good of the organization. Although the individual is hurt by this action, the lack of action will cause ten-fold damage to the organization. For the leader, it takes professional courage to make this call.

I consider it a courageous act because of how difficult it is to tell someone they are not making the grade. As a young officer, I can remember countless discussions at the bar about inept squadron commanders. Eventually the discussion would move to the question of why the wing commander could not see the same thing and fire the offender. Eventually, we would all make the statement if we were wing commanders, we would not allow inept commanders to ruin organizations. We would have the courage to make the tough call, and relieve the individual.

Once you become a wing commander, the task of relieving someone of their duty is not nearly as easy as it seemed back when you were a captain. First, most leaders develop a bond of loyalty with their subordinates, and are reluctant to relieve one unless the subordinate makes a major screw-up. Additionally, most leaders will not relieve a subordinate because they are not a great people person or fail to inspire respect. And in most cases, superiors will allow the subordinate to muddle through, looking forward to the time when he or she can be moved to another position.

You may ask why in the world would anyone select such an individual to lead. The answer is quite simple – you never know how an individual will perform as a leader until you give them the opportunity. Granted, you provide training, both academic and practical, prior to assuming a leadership position; but until the person is truly in the position, you have no idea how they'll do.

When #4 is #1

My first experience with having to demonstrate professional courage occurred when I was selected to be an F-15 squadron commander. My wing commander made a very unusual move – he allowed me to choose my operations officer. The operations officer is the second most influential person in the squadron after the commander. He runs the flying operation and sets the tone for the squadron.

I always believed my ops officer should be someone the young pilots respected, generated enthusiasm with a positive attitude and was an innovator. Additionally, I believed it important that the ops officer and commander respected each other and worked together as a team.

Although I appreciated the wing commander's offer, it placed me in a dilemma. Of the four officers to be considered, the one I wanted was #4 based on date of rank. In order for me to choose him, I would have to bypass the three other officers. Fortunately, another operations officer position was opening up so I would only have to bypass two officers.

The other new commander opted to take the most senior officer, even though he wasn't sure how that individual would perform. The other commander's rationale was that since he was senior, he deserved the opportunity. I did not necessarily disagree with that rationale. However, I felt that if you knew the individuals well enough, you owed it your organization to choose the best-qualified person to fill the job.

When I informed the wing commander of my choice, he wanted to know why I was passing over the other two officers. After he heard my explanations, he agreed with my rationale and supported my choice. As I was leaving his office, he stated to me that as a commander I had an obligation to explain to the two officers why I did not select either of them as my DO. Although I agreed, I did not look forward to the encounter.

Neither one of the officers was pleased with my decision, and wanted to know specifics as to why I thought they were not the best qualified. It's very uncomfortable to sit across from another individual and justify your decision for their non-selection by describing their shortcomings. The normal reaction by that individual is one of disbelief and shock followed by anger. But regardless of how uncomfortable it may be, it is the right thing to do and well worth it in the long run.

For the remainder of my tour, neither one of these officers spoke to me again. Although I hated having to have those discussions, once it had been done it was done and we all moved on. The officer chosen became an outstanding operations officer and a superb leader on the ground and in the air. As a team, we led our squadron to two consecutive selections as the best fighter squadron in Europe and went on to be selected as the best air superiority squadron in the Air Force. Without him by my side, I doubt the squadron would have reached this level of achievement. This experienced convinced me that the best approach is to pick the right person, and deal honestly with the non-selects no matter how uncomfortable it might be.

The Hardest Job

The most difficult decision I made during my many command tours involved relieving one of my operations group commanders – a full colonel. This officer was responsible for leading and managing three F-15 fighter squadrons. Unfortunately, he was neither trained nor prepared for this daunting task. The obvious question then is why would the Air Force place him in such a position? The answer is quite simple – the Air Force did not. A very influential four-star general forced the assignment.

In fairness, the officer was sharp and talented, but he had not been prepared through prior assignments for the demands of the Ops Group Commander job. He was a distinguished graduate of the Air Force Academy with an outstanding record of academic achievement. He went on to pilot training and a follow-on assignment to the training command as an instructor pilot.

He performed brilliantly. His next assignment was to an overseas F-15 squadron. Here he began to have problems. During his three-year tour, he spent his entire time in the safety office and only upgraded to two ship flight lead at the very end of his tour. In comparison, most of his peers moved from wingman to two ship flight lead to four ship flight lead to instructor pilot with jobs in scheduling, training, and weapons along the way.

After this tour, he went to a military educational institution where he once again excelled in the academic arena. After school, he moved on to a headquarters staff where he excelled as a staff officer. Unfortunately for him, at the conclusion of this assignment, instead of going back to flying, he went on to another school followed by another prestigious staff job at the Pentagon.

It was during this last tour that he was noticed by the four-star general. At the conclusion of his Pentagon assignment, the general insisted the officer be placed in an F-15 wing as the deputy group commander with a fly up to the commander's position within a year. Initially Air Combat Command resisted the assignment since the officer had not flown in nine years, and did not possess the flying proficiency required. However, the four-star general insisted and the officer was moved into the deputy group commander position.

When I assumed command of the wing, the officer had been on board for one year and was scheduled to assume command of the group the next week. During the previous year, his flying skills had not improved and he still was flying on the wing instead of being a flight lead. Although the squadron commanders and other pilots liked this officer, they did not respect him as a combat air leader because, quite simply, he wasn't one. Every commander under him, including his own deputy, were all four-ship flight leads with instructor pilot certification.

This situation troubled me. There was no doubt in my mind this officer was not suited for this particular leadership position, but at the same time I realized if I relieved him it was the end of a very promising career. Additionally, he had done nothing wrong. His entire career he had done what the Air Force had asked of him. The culprit in this case was the four-star who force fit a square peg into a round hole. I'm convinced that if this officer had been assigned to the training command he would have performed brilliantly and been selected for promotion to general. Unfortunately, this was not the case, and he was in my fighter wing and my challenge.

Trying to be fair, I decided I would let the officer assume command, but immediately placed the deputy in charge and sent the new commander to a squadron where his only job would be to fly everyday, sharpen his skills, and check out as a flight lead. I wasn't even going to demand he become a four-ship flight lead – two-ship would be acceptable. I just wanted him to occasionally lead his pilots instead of always flying on their wing.

Fortunately the officer appreciated my concerns, and eagerly began his focused, intense training program. At first, everything was going well – the officer had a great attitude and really applied himself. But, as he began to fly more demanding missions, he began to falter and have trouble. After four weeks of flying every day, and giving him the very best instruction available, I called in his instructors for an assessment. They were uneasy talking about their commander's flying ability with the wing commander. However, I impressed on them the need for absolute candor and objective assessment. After all, our wing deployed to Southwest Asia 180 days of every year, and it was quite possible this officer could take these pilots to combat. Was he qualified to lead them? Bottom line – *no*.

They all agreed that with another month of training he might be considered safe enough to lead, but certainly would never be competent enough to lead in training exercises like Red Flag or real combat. Although I had hoped with all my heart the officer would make it, I knew his chances were slim based on his experience and past performance in fighters.

I finally came to the conclusion that I had to relieve this officer. It was a very difficult decision for many reasons. First, I knew this would stop his progression, and end his career. There would be no more opportunities for command after this. Second, I knew there was no written Air Force requirement that the officer had to be able to lead a two-ship, but I knew that without that status, the officer would never be respected. Without respect, how can an officer lead?

The other factor that bothered me was that this officer had done nothing wrong – he had simply done what his Air Force told him to do. I am confident that if he had been assigned to a flying training wing where the flying leadership demands are not the same, he would have been very successful. However, because a four-star was determined to assign this officer to a job he was unprepared for, I now had to end what was a promising career.

Late one afternoon, I had the officer come to my office. In the next hour, I had one of the most difficult conversations of my career. I first outlined my concerns, then discussed his lack of progress in the special checkout program, and finally announced I could not keep him in a command position. Although I am sure he did not fully expect my action, he was not completely surprised.

He told me he knew he was having problems flying and was concerned about how that would affect his ability to lead. However, he felt with a few more training flights he could get to the level I expected. I appreciated his position but couldn't keep him in a special status until he finally got it. He needed to be leading his group now, not flying every day being trained like a young lieutenant. Sadly, he had his chance and had not been able to meet expectations.

The next part of our conversation really caught me off guard. I fully expected the officer to become defensive and possibly even rude to me. I imagine I probably would have – after all, I had just ended his career. Instead, the officer spent a few minutes letting me know how much he enjoyed working for me, the respect he had for me as a leader, that he had hoped to gain my confidence, and had hoped to one day lead a wing the way I did. He regretted he had failed in this endeavor, and respected me even more for the manner in which I handled the issue.

By the time he finished, I was on the verge of tears. Not because he had said so many positive things about me, but because of his immensely positive character and the fact I was doing a very bad thing to a very good person. Although my head was telling me I had made the right decision in a very difficult situation, my heart was calling me every despicable name you can imagine. As we parted, we shook hands and hugged – a very emotional moment for us both.

After the officer left, I began calling general officers at the headquarters to find the very best job I could for this officer. Given his superb staff skills, he was picked up and went on to do a great job for the Air Combat Command staff. Since we lived on the same base, I would occasional see him at various locations, and each and every time, he would approach me, warmly greet me, and engage in a friendly conversation. I was astounded at his apparent lack of bitterness toward me. As it turned out, he retired shortly thereafter and began a wonderful second career.

Although it pains me when I think of this event, I am still convinced it was the right thing to do. My first obligation as a commander is to my airmen – to lead and care for them and ensure commanders below me do the same. Granted, the wing could have propped up this officer for two years, but it would have been unfair to the officers and enlisted personnel who deserved a combat-ready leader and commander.

This was absolutely the toughest decision I had to make in my career. I stopped the progression of a very talented officer who certainly could have successfully commanded in the right organization. However, he was not in the right organization, and he was having a negative effect on my combat wing. Therefore, in my mind, I had no choice.

I replaced this officer with a highly respected F-15 pilot who possessed all the right credentials. He succeeded and the operations group performed magnificently during his tour. Throughout the remainder of my tour at Langley, I had many individuals express their appreciation and admiration for the action I took. Not because they disliked their former commander – on the contrary, they all liked him and regretted seeing him relieved. But they all realized he was not suited to command their organization and that in the best case the group would remain static, and in the worst, it may suffer losses in real world combat. I did not want to relieve this officer, and it took every ounce of professional courage I possessed to do the right thing.

In the private sector, these types of actions happen much more frequently because of mergers, a slow economy, profit loss, *etc*. However, the same lesson applies to business as it does to the military. Whenever you have someone unqualified in a leadership position, the organization will suffer until that person is removed. Although it may be very difficult to do, you must have the professional courage to confront the situation and deal with it squarely – either the individual gains the skill required, or the individual leaves.

Here is another area where followers expectations are fairly low for their leadership. After all, it is so much easier for a leader to just ignore or tolerate a subordinate's subpar performance, counting on others to take up the slack. Followers appreciate how difficult it is to relieve someone. Given the task, most followers would shirk this onerous duty as most leaders do.

When a leader steps up to this very difficult and anguishing task, followers take note. They understand the courage it takes and they appreciate that they're working for a unique leader – one who has the professional courage to do what is right for the organization and the followers regardless of personal hardship. This action on the leader's part not only exceeds expectations, it blows your followers away. In a world-class organization that seeks to exceed expectations, there is no room for an individual in a leadership position who cannot inspire, motivate, and lead from the front.

THE IMPORTANCE OF BALANCE

When I talk about priorities, I'm only really addressing two – the professional and the personal. I have observed many a great leader fail in these areas, and pay a heavy price for the choices they made. I believe the approach one must take is to balance the two and allow them to move back and forth as necessary. If life is normal for you, your friends and your family, then your job usually takes top billing. After all, we do have to make a living and provide for our loved ones. However, when unique events occur, then it may be necessary to move personal needs up front.

When a leader adopts a philosophy that allows and encourages followers to take a balanced approach to job and family, you would be amazed at how much that builds trust and confidence in the leader, and commitment from their organizational members. When the followers recognize their leader values them as people with families, and that their families are as important as the job, the followers begin to believe in the leader and the organization.

Now there are some that believe people will take advantage of their leader's kindness, understanding, and compassion. I will not dispute that this will happen, but not in great numbers. On the contrary, the vast majority of your people will form a bond with you and your organization and work even harder to exceed expectations. They begin to believe the organization cares about them as individuals and members of a family.

Leaders must appreciate when they make this commitment, people will come to them in time of need – whether it be for an unfortunate situation or the once in a lifetime event. If the request is indeed valid, the leader must not hesitate, but immediately deliver on the commitment to the workforce. If ever there is a denial or a reluctance to provide for a valid need, the word will quickly spread. When that happens, the trust and confidence that has been gained will be lost, and the leader will forever be viewed with suspicion by everyone in the organization.

I learned this valuable balanced approach to career and family when I was a young major working as an aide for a four-star general in Europe. Up until that time in my career, I believed my three priorities in life were my career, the airplane I flew, and my family – in that order. Fortunately my wife believed I would finally appreciate the need to balance these priorities and stayed with me through my early and immature years!

The four-star general firmly believed in the need for leadership to support the family. Whenever a valid need arose, he immediately provided the assistance required. This approach completely turned around the environment in our organization. My four-star had replaced an individual who cared very little about his people, and was more of a driver than a leader. Morale was low in the headquarters, and productivity was barely meeting the standard expected. Within months, morale was high and productivity began increasing. This outstanding work environment remained in place throughout the general's tenure.

When I assumed my first command, the 22nd Fighter Squadron, I adopted this same approach. It produced an organization that is still a legend in the Air Force today. The squadron went from the very worst in the Air Force to the top squadron in Europe and later, in the Air Force – all in two years. As I progressed in my leadership roles, I continued this same approach with respect to the mission and family. As always, the results were the same: increased productivity, high morale, and a sense the organization and leadership cared about people. The wings under my command received the highest effectiveness ratings in the Air Force, the numbered air force achieved the highest space launch success rate in Air Force history, and my acquisition center turned around the worst reputation in the Air Force to the best.

All this work was done by the wonderful people in our organization. *They* made it happen, *not* me. The talent and capability in each organization was always there, it just never had been tapped by a leadership style that valued the worker's family as much as the worker's productivity.

Now with this approach comes a requirement for the leader to adopt the same approach with their personal priorities. If you're always the first in the office, the last to leave, work weekends, only take a vacation when forced, and leave all the family events to your spouse then you will be an abject failure with this approach. Remember, your people will base their behavior off yours – when they see your family is definitely the second or last priority, they will realize your pronouncements regarding the importance of the family are hollow.

I'm not suggesting you shouldn't work hard, take vacation or never miss a family event. This is unrealistic and as the leader, you will find yourself out of a leadership position very quickly. There must also be a balance in your life that is obvious to your people. When they see that, then they'll believe you practice what you preach.

I have seen many fine leaders fail to see the need for balance in their priorities. When the time comes to finally leave the job and spend time with the family, the family is no longer there. If you gain the world but lose your family in the process, you've likely gained nothing and lost everything.

Throughout my career, after learning this approach, I also took time to "smell the roses" with my family. It never hurt my advancement, and I'm convinced it sent the right signal to my workforce. I only had one real personal challenge to this approach during the twenty-plus years I used it.

The Fini Flight

I had just been promoted to brigadier general and reassigned to command the crown jewel of our fighter force – the 1st Fighter Wing. The change of command was in early May so I opted to leave my family behind in Florida for a month while my oldest daughter completed high school. The plan was for me to return the first week in June, attend her graduation, and then move the family to Virginia.

Around the end of May, I received a call from my public affairs officer wanting to brief me on the ceremony being set up for the retirement of the four-star commander of Air Combat Command (ACC). ACC was the biggest command in the Air Force and was headquartered at Langley. As the commander of Langley, my wing provided all the support the headquarters needed in order to run the command.

As you can imagine, the retirement was going to be a big event with almost a week of activities. The retiring four-star was a popular commander and everyone wanted to send him off in style. He had been particularly good to me by giving me two wings to command and was instrumental in my promotion to general. I liked him a lot and was willing to do almost anything to make the retirement events very special.

One of the events planned was a long-held tradition in the flying air force – the fini-flight. On this final flight, the person who is departing, either moving to a next assignment or retiring, is allowed to fly a mission of their choice with pilots of their choosing. When the mission is complete, and the aircraft have taxied back to their parking spot a fire truck is waiting to hose down the departing pilot. Additionally, there is a great gathering of friends, fellow pilots, spouses, and children to witness this event.

We had a fantastic fini-flight scheduled for the retiring general and I was to be in the flight and a major participant in the events that were to happen after we landed. Unfortunately, there was one big problem – the fini-flight was scheduled on the day my daughter was to graduate from high school in Florida. It would be absolutely impossible to participate in the event and also make my daughter's graduation.

Although I really respected the four-star for the great opportunities he had given me, there really was no choice. This was my daughter, and she was going to only graduate from high school once and she expected and wanted her dad there.

When I let the headquarters' staff know that I would be unable to participate in the fini-flight events there was much consternation. They were absolutely convinced that I was making the wrong decision and that I just had to be there. After all, it's just a high school graduation. True, but it was *my* daughter's high school graduation.

As the days passed, I got more and more calls about whether or not I really thought it was wise to miss the four-star's last flight. From the staff's perspective, the 1st Fighter Wing Commander just had to fly in the mission, and be there to welcome the four-star back and say some words about his great leadership to the assembled masses. I was convinced either my vice or one of the general officers on the headquarters staff could take my place.

I finally told the staff I planned to attend my daughter's graduation, and unless I got a direct order from a two or three-star general on the headquarters staff, that was the end of it. I never heard anymore about it. There's no doubt in my mind the four-star would have wanted me to be at my daughter's graduation instead of his fini-flight.

Throughout this entire ordeal, my staff was aware of what was going on between the headquarters staff and me. They also had heard in my commander's call earlier that month about my approach to balancing the job and the family. No doubt they were wondering if I would follow the approach I had outlined for the airmen. It did not take long for the word to travel throughout the wing that the new commander was not going to participate in the fini-flight because he chose to attend his daughter's graduation.

When I returned from my daughter's graduation everything was fine. The fini-flight had been a great success and the four-star had a wonderful time. And just as I thought, when it was all over, he never said "I wonder where Bill Looney is? It just isn't the same without him..."

Too often leaders assume their personal involvement is so critical to every facet of the organization and every individual event that they can never be absent – *not true*. There are times where you can be absent and the organization will do just fine. Accept that and then live your life appropriately. The message you send to your people will be powerful. I can not tell you how many times during the next couple of months after that fini-flight, people would stop me and tell me how impressed they were that I went to my daughter's graduation and put my family first. Their comments not only reinforced my belief in this approach, but also put more credibility in my reply when I told them I wanted them to do the same thing.

Most followers expect leaders to only care about successful mission accomplishment. From their perspective, it is the rare leader who truly cares about the families of the workers. Not to say that all leaders fail to express verbally how much they care, it's just the actions of so many leaders are not in sync with their words. As the old saying goes: it's hard to hear what you are saying when your actions are so much louder than your words.

There are two ways you demonstrate to your people you care about their families. First, when confronted with an opportunity to support the family, take full advantage of it. Whether it be granting time off during a difficult situation, celebrating a family member's accomplishment, or being present for a unique event, do not let these opportunities pass you by.

Second, and just as importantly, value your own family as much as you say you value the workforce's families. If they see that your family has a low priority in your life, it will be hard for them to accept your commitment to theirs. Balance your family and your career – be there for the high and low times, and make sure your actions reflect your stated beliefs of how important family is.

When you do this, it will send a message through the entire organization that you mean what you say. Most importantly, through your actions, not your words, you will exceed expectations and fuel a commitment from your followers to you and your organization that will astound you.

Final Thoughts

Exceeding expectations is what sets people apart. Those who do on a consistent basis will be the ones who find the most success. For a leader to exceed expectations, it doesn't require any special physical attributes, extraordinary level of intelligence, or unique artistic skill. What it *does* require is someone who has a vision of where to take an organization and also how to take care of the workers while on this journey. Leaders do this by identifying with the workers and conducting themselves in a manner that does not expect special treatment. In other words, their actions demonstrate that it is all about the followers and their leader's commitment to their well-being. Being a humble, empathetic leader will ensure you not only meet but exceed this expectation.

Another requirement for a leader to exceed expectations is to create a culture to do exactly that. It starts by leading from the front and showing the workers that the leader not only understands what it takes to do the job, but can do the job as well. By leading from the front, the leader sets the example from the smallest task to ones that are encumbered with risk and difficulty. Never ask someone to go where you have not gone first.

A leader must appreciate that an organization that exceeds expectations is based on standards that allow every follower to reach their highest potential. It is up to the leader to enforce those standards, no matter the hardship or cost, so that the organization remains strong and vibrant. There will be difficult situations encountered in this regard. As a leader you must stand up and be counted. Do not shrink from your responsibilities to the organization.

Including others in creating the organization and working the issues is a must for the leader. Followers often do not expect to be included, and this simple gesture can pay huge dividends. The organization becomes stronger with more ideas from more people which then fosters buy-in and commitment by everyone involved.

Do not allow individuals who cannot lead to lead. A leader has an obligation to the followers to provide the best possible leadership at all levels. When that is not happening, the leader must have the courage to take the action required no matter the individual pain and anguish caused. This is not normal human behavior, but it is the only way to ensure an organization will exceed expectations along with its leader.

A leader must focus on his or her own personal behavior. The manner in which they conduct themselves will always speak volumes about who they really are versus what they say or write. A leader must maintain the highest standards and level of integrity. There is no room for even the slightest hint of deceit or devious behavior. Followers expect perfection and leaders must deliver.

Leaders must always be positive. For if not you, then who? Followers are looking for you to believe there is a way – even in the darkest of times. As Winston Churchill said, "*Never, never, never, never, never give up!*" Yes, some of your followers will, but even when they do they still do not expect you to give up. Stay positive, believe there is a way, find it, and lead your followers to it.

Never forget how important family is – to you and your followers. Without a commitment to a balance between career and family, it will be hard for followers to truly believe their leader cares about anything but mission accomplishment and personal success. Living this belief with one's own family is also the only way to make this commitment come alive. By exceeding expectations in this area, the leader will tee up all the other areas for the same result.

Creating an organization that exceeds expectations is not that difficult. Unfortunately, my experience has shown me that most followers expect their leaders to be self-absorbed and self-serving – sad but true. Given such an expectation, it is possible for every leader to create an organizational culture where exceeding expectations is the norm. It's not that hard, but it takes a commitment to your people, your organization, and yourself. It's understanding that leadership is all about the followers not the leaders, and then demonstrating that appreciation through your every action. Understand, appreciate, and live this philosophy as a leader and both you and your organization will *exceed expectations*.

ACKNOWLEDGMENTS

Many thanks to Jim Parco and Dave Levy for their vision, foresight, and encouragement as I went through the process of turning an idea into a reality. Their personal involvement took this book to a much higher level and I thank them for their hard work, long hours, and unwavering commitment to this effort. Additionally, I appreciate the outstanding efforts of Paul Hoffman and two anonymous reviewers for their thorough reviews and insightful comments. Finally, to Joel Martinez and Deanne Driver whose artistic talents did wonders for the cover.

ABOUT THE AUTHOR

General Bill Looney retired from the United States Air Force as a four-star General having served for forty years. He graduated from the Air Force Academy in 1972 where he was the Cadet Wing Commander. General Looney eventually command-ed more organizations than any other Air Force general officer in history, with each organization he led achieving demonstrable higher levels of performance and productivity. He is a highly-decorated officer with over 4,200 flying hours. He and his wife, Marilyn, have two daughters, two sons-in-law, both Air Force officers, and two grandchildren.

CPSIA information can be obtained at www.ICGtesting.com
Printed in the USA
268510BV00004B/16/P